Whatever seems beautiful we made by the grace of God

PLEASURE OF RUINS

16 Plates in Color
140 Monochrome Plates
26 Maps and Plans

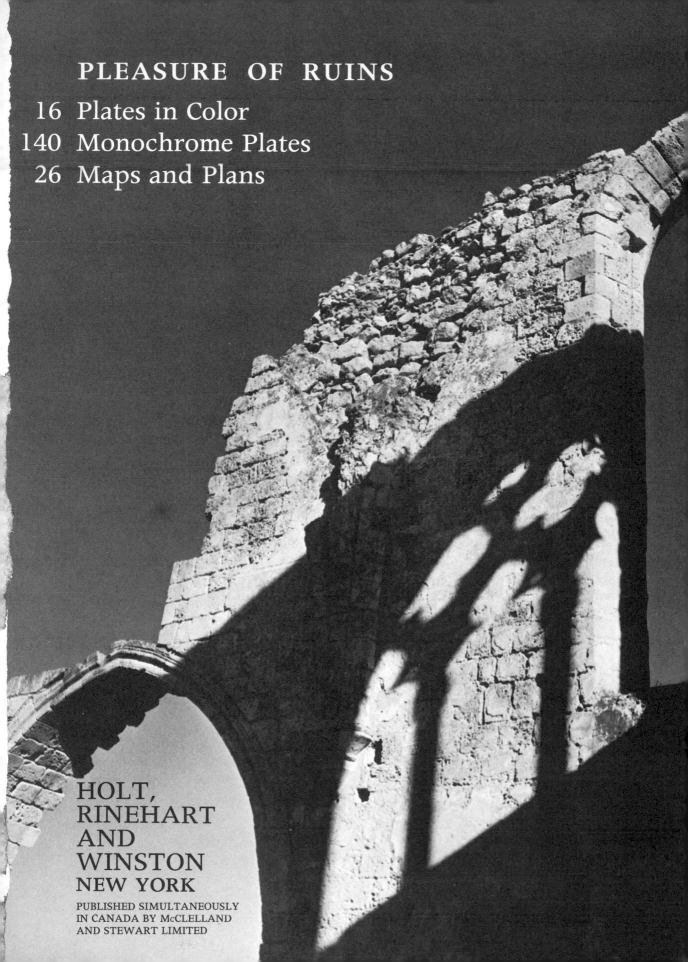

HOLT,
RINEHART
AND
WINSTON
NEW YORK

PUBLISHED SIMULTANEOUSLY
IN CANADA BY McCLELLAND
AND STEWART LIMITED

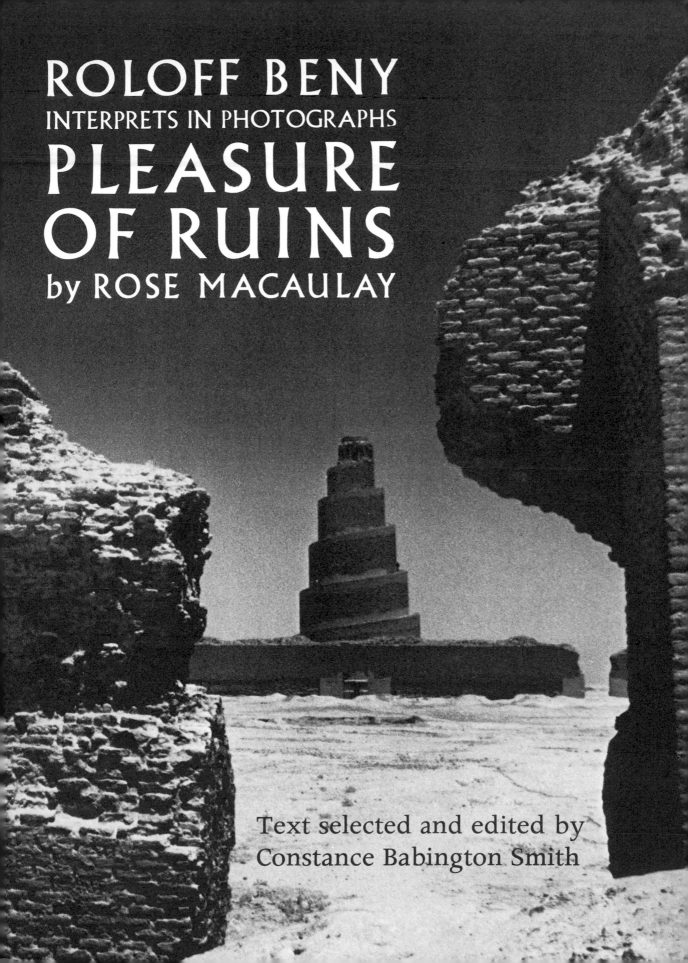

ROLOFF BENY
INTERPRETS IN PHOTOGRAPHS
PLEASURE
OF RUINS
by ROSE MACAULAY

Text selected and edited by
Constance Babington Smith

Contents

This is a revised edition of *Pleasure of Ruins* by Rose Macaulay, interpreted in photographs by Roloff Beny, which was first published in 1964. The first edition of Rose Macaulay's *Pleasure of Ruins* was published in 1953

© 1964 and 1977 Thames and Hudson Ltd © 1964 and 1977 Text of *Pleasure of Ruins* Constance Babington Smith

Library of Congress Catalog Card Number: 77-71369
ISBN: 0-03-021091-7
10 9 8 7 6 5 4 3 2 1

Color plates printed in the Netherlands by Drukkerij de Lange/van Leer, Deventer and London
Text and monochrome illustrations printed in Great Britain by BAS Printers Limited, Over Wallop, Hampshire

The cuneiform inscription facing the half-title page was carved four times on the Propylaea of Xerxes I at Persepolis. The half-title page shows the Church of the Carmelites, Famagusta, Cyprus. The title page shows the Mosque of Mutawakkil, Samarra, Iraq.

For John — without double entendre, but with double love

Contents

The sources of the plans are as follows: Ephesus, Jerash, Palmyra, Pergamum, Petra and Spalato: Swan's Hellenic Cruises, Handbook for 1963 *(courtesy W. F. and R. K. Swan (Hellenic) Ltd); Rievaulx Abbey:* Rievaulx Abbey, *by the late Sir Charles Peers (by permission of the Controller of Her Majesty's Stationery Office, Crown Copyright reserved); Anuradhapura:* Handbook for Travellers in India and Pakistan, 19th edition *(courtesy John Murray Ltd). The remaining plans have been adapted from the work of the following authorities: Adina Mosque (Ravenshaw); Angkor (B. Groslier and J. Arthaud); Antioch (L. Bakalowits after G. Rey); Chichen Itza, Copan (Tatiana Proskouriakoff); Crac des Chevaliers (G. Rey); Ellora (J. Fergusson and J. Burgess); Firuzabad (A. Upham Pope); Fountains Abbey (J. Arthur Reeve); Goa (J. N. da Fonseca); Halebid (J. Fergusson); Leptis Magna (D. Haynes); Persepolis (Ali Hakemi of the Iranian Archaeological Service); Stokesay (J. A. Gotch); St Hilarion (Antiquities Department of the Government of Cyprus).*

on his 50th birthday!
David and Christian

Introduction

The approach to ruins in this highly selective book will be seen to be that of a pleasurist. It is not architectural or archaeological, nor in any other way expert. Its aim, however incoherently kept in view and inadequately achieved, is to explore the various kinds of pleasure given to various people at various epochs by the spectacle of ruined buildings. Here and there ... I have made some attempt to trace the growth and development of this strange human reaction to decay. Elsewhere the emphasis is on the ruins themselves, and the impression they individually make, by their beauty, or their strangeness, or their shattered intimidations that strike so responsive a nerve in our destruction-seeking souls. Or, more usually, by their mere picturesqueness. 'I am living in the Capuchin Convent,' Byron wrote from Athens, 'Hymettus before me, the Acropolis behind, the Temple of Jove to my right, the Stadium in front, the town to my left; eh, Sir, there's a situation, there's your picturesque!' Or, as Marie Lloyd used to sing, 'I am very fond of ruins, ruins I love to scan.' That is the common human sentiment; when did it consciously begin, this delight in decayed or wrecked buildings? Very early it seems. Since down the ages men have meditated before ruins, rhapsodized before them, mourned pleasurably over their ruination, it is interesting to speculate on the various strands in this complex enjoyment, on how much of it is admiration for the ruin as it was in its prime – *quanta Roma fuit, ipsa ruina docet* – how much aesthetic pleasure in its present appearance – *plus belle que la beauté est la ruine de la beauté* – how much is association, historical or literary, what part is played by morbid pleasure in decay, by righteous pleasure in retribution (for so often it is the proud and the bad who have fallen), by mystical pleasure in the destruction of all things mortal and the eternity of God (a common reaction in the Middle Ages), by egotistic satisfaction in surviving – (where now art thou? here still am I) – by masochistic joy in a common destruction – *L'homme va méditer sur les ruines des empires, il oublie qu'il est lui-même une ruine encore plus chancelante, et qu'il sera tombé avant ces débris* – and by a dozen other entwined threads of pleasurable and melancholy emotion, of which the main strand is, one imagines, the romantic and conscious swimming down the hurrying river of time, whose mysterious reaches, stretching limitlessly behind, glimmer suddenly into view with these wracks washed on to the silted shores. More

intellectual than any of these emotions are those two learned, noble and inquisitive pleasures, archaeology and antiquarianism, which have inspired so much eager research, such stalwart, patient and prolonged investigation, such ingenious and erroneous deductions and reconstructions, and have been rewarded by those exquisite thrills of triumph and discovery which must be as exciting as finding a new land. These are, no doubt, the highest and purest of ruin-pleasures, but are reserved for the few.

Then there is the host of minor pleasures – looting, carrying away fragments (a treat enjoyed by great looters and small, from Lord Elgin and the Renaissance nobles and popes to the tourist pocketing stone eggs from fallen Corinthian capitals). There is the pleasure of constructing among the ruins a dwelling or a hermitage (for the enterprising and eccentric company of the Stylites, this is apt to be on the tops of pillars), of being portrayed against a ruinous background (very large, the ruins very small, as William Lithgow before Troy, and Goethe seated on a fallen column in the Campagna), of writing or cutting one's name, as all good tourists have done in all times, of self-projection into the past, of composing poetry and prose, of observing the screech owl, the bat, and the melancholy ghost, and the vegetation that pushes among the crevices and will one day engulf.

Whatever its complex elements, the pleasure felt by most of us in good ruins is great. 'A monument of antiquity', wrote Thomas Whately in 1770, 'is never seen with indifference. . . . No circumstance so forcibly marks the desolation of a spot once inhabited, as the prevalence of Nature over it.' *Jam seges est ubi Troja fuit* is a sentence which conveys a stronger idea of a city totally overthrown, than a description of its remains. We might be still more delighted to see Troy or Athens, Corinth, Paestum or Rome, as they stood two thousand odd years ago; but that cannot be; this broken beauty is all we have of that ancient magnificence; we cherish it like the extant fragments of some lost and noble poem.

Unthinking ἰδιῶται, unversed in their own emotions, not knowing that they love ruins, reveal it not in words, but by continually making more of them; more and more and more. This book is a random excursion into the fantastic world that the ἰδιῶται (including Time, their chief) have made and left, a shattered heritage, for us to deplore and to admire. Many of the ruins here mentioned I have seen, many not. Some I have not seen for many years, and since I saw them they have suffered change. Ruins change so fast that one cannot keep pace: they disintegrate, they go to earth, they are tidied up, excavated, cleared of vegetation, built over, restored, prostrate columns set on end and fitted with their own or other capitals; fresh areas of ancient cities are exposed, scattered ruins assembled together in railed enclosures, ruin-squatting populations expelled from castles and abbeys, walls repaired. Even between typing and printing, printing and publication, drastic changes in ruins everywhere occur; one cannot keep pace. One must select for contemplation some phase in a ruin's devious career, it matters little which, and consider the human reaction to this; or merely enjoy one's own.

'A heartless pastime', Henry James called his own ruin-questing (and this was a title I considered for my book), 'and the pleasure, I confess, shows a note of perversity.' Indeed, I fear this may seem to many a perverse book. For, out of this extremely ruinous world (in which there are, above and under the earth, far more ruined than unruined buildings), I have only had space to select a few ruinous objects, a ruin here and a ruin there, to illustrate the human attitude towards them, and the odds are against anyone's finding here more than a few of their own favourite ruins. I have not attempted to deal with all types of ruin; I have, for instance, no separate sections for theatres, forums, aqueducts, arches, baths or bridges, each of which could have filled long chapters; but they have had to come in, all too cursorily, with the rest; and a chapter to be called 'Mouldering Mansions' never got past a rough draft. Still, it may be held that this book, whatever it lacks, does not suffer from brevity, so perhaps it is for the best.

ROSE MACAULAY

Jerash, Jordan. Capitals by the Western Baths

Preface

Rose Macaulay's gift for enjoying—her zest for finding interest or amusement in almost everything—was one of her most endearing qualities. It also inspired no less than three of her books. In her anthology *The Minor Pleasures of Life* she gathered together the enjoyments of others, from Cicero to Jane Austen; then in *Personal Pleasures* she told, in lighthearted vein, of her own exceedingly varied tastes and addictions. Finally, in *Pleasure of Ruins*, she struck out into new depths, combining her theme of the pleasurable with that of ruination, a subject which for a time came to dominate her thinking almost to the point of obsession. For in her complex character, unsuspected by those who knew her only as a brilliantly witty novelist, there was a sensitivity to the darkness of despair. The devastation of the Second World War, the ruins of lives as well as of bomb-shattered buildings (including those of her own home in London), became to her a terrible symbol of spiritual dereliction. To those with eyes to see, this is proclaimed in her novel *The World my Wilderness*, which was written just after the war.

In 1949 she began to write 'a short book on the pleasure of looking at ruins', as she described it at the time. Once more Pleasure kindled her, and she became so fascinated by her researches, as she found more and more delightful ruins and ruin-lovers, all through the ages and all over the world, that *Pleasure of Ruins* eventually proved to be the longest book she had ever written. She worked on it for over four years, and visited quite a number of the sites, but she did not go further afield than the Middle East. Her travels nearly always drew her towards Mediterranean countries, which she loved very dearly, especially Italy, where the happiest years of her childhood had been spent.

Not long before her death in 1958 she told me (we were cousins, and became close friends towards the end of her life) that she was composing an essay on Mediterranean ruins for a book of 'beautiful photographs'. The book was *The Thrones of Earth and Heaven*; the photographs were by Roloff Beny. Later, when after her death I was editing a book of her letters, I wrote to Mr Beny because I was eager for his permission to include a photograph he had taken of Dame Rose in a garden in Venice. I mentioned that since her death I had become responsible for decisions concerning her writings. Soon it came to light that they had often talked of combining photographs by him with selections from *Pleasure of Ruins* to form a pictorial edition of the book. We both felt that the idea should be developed, and I agreed to undertake the editing of the text.

My aim in the editing has been to preserve the spirit and scope of the original, in spite of the fact that the two books are necessarily different in character, and that very drastic selectiveness has been unavoidable. As Rose Macaulay herself wrote in her *Personal Pleasures*: 'Had I but world enough and time, I might have continued this agreeable pastime for ever. There are a thousand pleasures, even of my own, left unrecorded in this brief choice. But a choice it had to be, owing, as I say, to this perhaps fortunate limitation of world and time which sets so brief a term to all our undertakings.'

CONSTANCE BABINGTON SMITH

11

Great cities decline, they gradually submit to history, caught in the organic grip of nature and left haunted, or cruelly stripped of embellishments by man's urge to plunder. Some vanish; of those that remain, the ruins are often more majestic and, paradoxically, more human. Palaces of Persian kings, Roman and Byzantine emperors, of Sassanian caliphs and Haitian usurpers; Cistercian abbeys, Doric temples, tombs, Norman towers, Mogul domes and Gothic spires all suffer the same torment, but in their deserted royal parks, in shadowed jungles—some slowly melting back into the desert, others silently dissolving under water—the mystery of their vanished past glory fills the aware observer with awe and respect. The photographs in this book, chosen after much deliberation from many hundreds, will I hope convey something of the magic I felt when confronted by these remnants of man's purpose.

My copy of *Pleasure of Ruins*, now battered and travel-stained, had been my constant companion for nine years. I had been dedicating a good part of my waking dreams to an almost predestined pursuit of the itineraries explored by Rose Macaulay, whose experiences I had vicariously enjoyed and whose inspired prose had given me continuous pleasure. But it was only in 1962, through the graciousness of her heirs, that the words of this 'passionate sightseer' and my own images of her 'phantom towns' were commissioned in book form, even though I had often discussed it with Dame Rose during the last seven years of her life. The challenge, then, came not as a surprise but as an intoxicating inevitability.

The minimum task I set myself required exploring and establishing aesthetic rapport with 140 archaeological sites and historical monuments in thirty-eight countries. In effect, insuperable difficulties prevented me from visiting a few of the places envisaged when the book was planned. In place of these I have, with Constance Babington Smith's concurrence, included several exceptional sites, which I made a point of seeking out because they complement Dame Rose's descriptions though she did not specifically mention them.

To undertake so complex an itinerary, which follows partly the path of Alexander the Great and partly that traced and retraced by Marco Polo—and even beyond, to the China coast in the east and the Pacific coast of South America in the west—necessitated my going alone. I set out from Rome in October 1962 for Central America, not to return until I descended at Leonardo da Vinci airport, twelve months and 137 take-offs later. In that interval I endured extremes of temperature, jeeps, beasts and antiquated aircraft, viruses, bureaucratic officials, strange languages, beds, religions and currencies, while I balanced precariously on an ephemeral rainbow of pleasures.

Now, looking down from my terrace on the Tiber, I think of the other rivers of the world, rivers which dictated the location of many of the fallen cities which I have explored. And, as I look beyond the river to the Palatine Hill, I recall the unearthly dawns and dusks: I see majestic ruins even in the architecture of the skies.

ROLOFF BENY

ACKNOWLEDGMENTS

This book would not have been realized without the help of many hundreds of individuals who in one way or another gave me their time and the benefit of their knowledge, encouraged me when I despaired of ever reaching my goal, and offered me hospitality and friendship throughout my odyssey. To all of them I should like to express my deepest gratitude for their invaluable contribution.

R. B.

---

1 The stupendous past

LOST SPLENDOUR

The ascendancy over men's minds of the ruins of the stupendous past, the past of history, legend and myth, at once factual and fantastic, stretching back and back into ages that can but be surmised, is half-mystical in basis. The intoxication, at once so heady and so devout, is not the romantic melancholy engendered by broken towers and mouldered stones; it is the soaring of the imagination into the high empyrean where huge episodes are tangled with myths and dreams; it is the stunning impact of world history on its amazed heirs. Such ascendancy has been swayed down the ages by the ruins of Troy, of Crete, Mycenae, Tyre, Nineveh, Babylon, Thebes, Rome, Byzantium, Carthage, and every temple, theatre and broken column of classical Greece; it is less ruin-worship than the worship of a tremendous past. . . .

The ghosts of Nineveh and Babylon, those mighty cities gone down into the immensities of the desert, have haunted men's minds with a sense of fearful hugeness, with their winged man-headed bulls guarding majestic gates, their improbable Assyrian grandeur. Vanished Assyria is no part of our western heritage; its ruins, uncovered, speak of an alien world in alien tongues; they stun us with aloof astonishment; Sennacherib and Sargon, Nebuchadnezzar and his court, seem as strange and remote as the winged bulls themselves. Not there, as in Greece, do we meet the legends and the myths we know; the ghosts that haunt those deserts are not the familiars of our childhood tales. . . . A different, less sensuous and facile, more purely imaginative type of pleasure is offered by the remains of Nineveh and Babylon. Petra, Palmyra, and Baalbek can be enjoyed by anyone with eyes. Nineveh and Babylon need imagination, and some knowledge. To put it bluntly, they are, in fact, little more than mounds.

Sir A. H. Layard, Nineveh's pioneer excavator, drew the distinction a century ago. No use, he pointed out, crossing the Euphrates to seek such ruins in Mesopotamia and Chaldaea as one finds in Syria and Asia Minor. Not here the graceful columns rising above myrtle, ilex and oleander, the amphitheatre covering a gentle slope and overlooking a lake-like, dark blue bay; not here the richly carved cornice or capital among luxuriant foliage; instead, the stern, shapeless mound rising like a hill from the scorched plain, the stupendous mass of brickwork occasionally laid bare by winter rains. . . .

No great city had ever gone more utterly underground than the huge ancient capital of Assyria since its destruction in the seventh century BC. Its ruins crumbled gradually; as they covered a space of many miles it was before long impossible to identify the site of the actual city; and which were the ruins seen by Cyrus's army as it marched by them in the fifth century, is doubtful. The whole business of Nineveh is confused. . . . By the nineteenth century, the great sprawling plain of city, suburbs, gardens and parks that lay along the Tigris opposite the town of Mosul was silted over by desert, and only mounds indicated where walls, palaces and ramparts stood. . . .

There is no more zestful narration in the exciting history of archaeology than Layard's of his excavations of Nineveh and Nimrud. . . . For Layard was that imaginative and enterprising being, an archaeologist, to whom a shapeless mound in Mesopotamia suggested limitless discoveries, infinite pleasures and palaces through which he might roam. And so it turned out. . . . He found walls carved with bas-reliefs of a period belonging to the second Assyrian empire; there were human figures, gods, warriors, kings, animals, flowers, eagle-headed men, winged bulls, human-headed lions, adorning the chambers of palaces of the ninth century BC. After a particularly sensational find – two huge human-headed winged lions – Layard . . . delighted with their grand appearance, contemplated them for hours; he thought they looked noble and sublime, and the reflection that they had been, perhaps, hidden from the eye of man for twenty-five centuries overwhelmed him. . . .

As many bas-reliefs of winged lions, bulls and kings as anyone could wish turned up; sphinxes too, and a black marble obelisk. The Arabs entered into the work with zest; Layard gave them frequent feasts and dances, and his enthusiasm was shared by all. . . . Every day turned up richly-carved bas-reliefs of figures, animals, monsters, sacred trees, and scenes of solemn ritual or adventure. The life they indicated was one of hunting, battle, religious ceremonies celebrated by king and priest, and the participation in all these activities of winged creatures of dubious biological category. The Arabs were highly interested in these figures, greeting them with extravagant gestures and cries of surprise. The bearded men they distrusted, believing them to be idols of jinns. The eunuchs they took for beautiful females, and kissed or patted them on the cheek. Excited by each fresh find they would rush like madmen into the trenches, throwing off their clothes and shouting the war-cry of their tribe. . . .

'Is not Nineveh most delightful and prodigious?' wrote a young lady to her brother in India. 'Papa says nothing so truly thrilling has happened in excavations since they found Pompeii.' Nor, on the whole, had it. Visitors flocked out to see it; archaeologists wrote books reconstructing the palaces; more and more year by year was uncovered. Many travellers, rashly braving the Assyrian summer, succumbed to fever; recovering and returning home, they half-suspected that the strange underground world they had seen had been part of their delirium.

More than ever they might think so today, standing on the bare, unrewarding mounds of Kouyunjik and Nimrud, with the desert spreading round, and nothing to hint at buried palaces except ridges and trenched earth, and, at Nimrud, here and there a fragment of a winged bull (those creatures so little lovable to any but Assyrians) pushing up a bearded head, to be made a target for the shots of British marksmen. . . .

Pilgrims to Nineveh must rely now on the pleasures of imagination. They can roam about the mounds, treading on twenty centuries of Assyrian history; they can quote Zephaniah the prophet, who, like all prophets, rejoiced over the ruin of great cities, confident that they had richly deserved their fate, for prophets have believed all large cities to be given over to wickedness and an abomination in the eyes of the Lord, and no doubt they are right. They have been the most single-minded of ruin-lovers, having no use for cities until they fall, and then rejoicing over the shattered remains in ringing words.

And he will stretch out his hand against the north, and destroy Assyria, and will make Nineveh a desolation, and dry like a wilderness. . . . the cormorant and the bittern shall lodge in the upper lintels of it; their voice shall sing in the windows; desolation shall be in the thresholds. . . . This is the rejoicing city that dwelt carelessly, that said in her heart, I am, and there is none beside me: how is she become a desolation, a place for beasts to lie down in! every one that passeth by her shall hiss, and wag his hand.

It may be questioned if Zephaniah would have approved the excavations which have brought the wicked palaces to light, to be marvelled at by future generations who neither hiss nor wag their hands, but carefully steal decorations and graven images and store them in museums for the admiration of the world.

Babylon, too, that 'golden cup in the Lord's hand, that made all the earth drunken', Babylon 'shall become heaps, a dwelling place for dragons, an astonishment and an hissing, without an inhabitant'; neither shall the Arabian pitch tent there, but wild beasts of the desert shall lie there, and their houses shall be full of doleful creatures, and owls shall dwell there and satyrs shall dance there, and the wild beasts of the islands shall cry in their desolate houses, and dragons in their pleasant palaces.

Thus the triumphing Jewish prophets, starting the career of the ruined Babylon with the sensational press that it has maintained ever since. For Babylon, unlike Nineveh, has always been much visited and described in her ruin. The curious thing about her visitors is the dissimilarity of the accounts they have from the first given, almost as if they had seen different ruins. The Hebrew Prophets, those grandiosely fantasticating ruin-builders, contrived owls, dragons, dancing satyrs in the pleasant palaces, every macabre circumstance of ruined cities that ruin-lovers have in all ages devised and sought. They liked to picture the resplendent edifices as caves for howling beasts, the temples and palaces hissing with serpents, the hanging gardens, once the wonder of the world, now its trample and spurn. It grieved them to see, half a century after the destruction of the wicked old Babylon by Sennacherib, a new Babylon arise, more resplendent, and very probably more wicked, than the old, to grow wealthier and more magnificent than all the cities of Asia and Egypt, not excepting Thebes. They must have been disappointed that Cyrus when he conquered it did not destroy it, but cherished and embellished it and made it a great Persian city. . . . Darius, and after him Xerxes, apparently wrought more destruction, but even this cannot have come up to prophetic standards, for Herodotus, describing Babylon fifty years later, mentions the walls and the great temple of Belus and other buildings and towers as being there in his time. Ruin is always overstated; it is part of the ruin-drama staged perpetually in the human imagination, half of whose desire is to build up, while the other half smashes and levels to the earth.

Alexander, entering Babylon a century after Herodotus wrote, found it still a fine city, though, according to Arrian and Strabo, much of it . . . lay buried in rubbish that it would have taken ten thousand workmen two months to clear. Accounts as usual, differ; one is inclined, from experience, to believe the less ruinous and spectacular. . . .

After the beginning of the Christian era, tourists (who continued assiduously to visit or pass it) were of many minds about its precise condition. Eusebius in the third century thought it completely a desert, Jerome in the fourth had a notion that the walls had been repaired and enclosed a park of game which the Persian kings hunted . . . Procopius in the sixth that it had for a long time been completely destroyed, Ibn Haukal in the tenth that it was a small village, Benjamin of Tudela in the twelfth that 'it now lies in ruins, but the streets extend thirty miles. . . .' Pietro della Valle in 1616 got, as might be expected, to the right place, and was the first visitor to describe the ruins as a mound, a heap, a mountain of confused débris. He saw a high, irregular mass of varying heights, built of bricks, with no shape to indicate particular buildings, though he thought that he identified the Tower of Babel. All that was visible to him of Babylon was this mountain of confusion, and it was difficult to believe that the proud city had stood on the site. His account is interesting as being the first to show Babylon going or gone to earth; henceforth it was what Jeremiah had called 'heaps'. . . .

The confusion of visitors on the spot was reflected by complete ignorance on the part of the untravelled,

> But where is lordly Babylon? where now
> Lifts she to heaven her giant brow?

the poet John Hughes inquired, and remained unanswered. During the next half-century, however, Babylonian travellers became more precise in their identifications.

Henceforth archaeologists took up in earnest the task of identifying the different mounds; it is when ruins have gone underground that research into them eagerly begins. Finally the German excavations, begun fifty years ago, scientifically and thoroughly uncovered what remained of a city used as a building quarry for some two thousand years. What was revealed was the New Babylon, the Babylon of Nebuchadnezzar and Belshazzar; of the more ancient city destroyed by Sennacherib practically nothing remained. Nebuchadnezzar's palaces . . . the temples, the walls, the gates, the quays, the great citadel, the Sacred Way, were unearthed, labelled, argued over, mapped and planned, written about, admired by countless visitors, covered up, and only excavated again lately; now one can see the Ishtar Gate and a mass of broken, clay-brick walls, and pick up enamelled bricks from the great processional way. Though it still looks a mess, it now repays a visit.

Apart from excavations, Babylon has its rewards. The view over the undulating, ruin-strewn desert, with its shifting colours in the changing light, the long city site lying along the palm-fringed Euphrates, the waters of Babylon; the knowledge that among and underneath the mounds lies the jumbled débris that was three thousand years ago the greatest city of the world, the capital of the Assyrian and Babylonish empires, should be enough for the romantic ruin-fancier. Travellers no longer think they see the Tower of Babel rising among the lesser ruins; but still they can enjoy the familiar meditations on fallen cities . . . can unite themselves . . . with the triumph of Alexander, riding into Babylon, his conquered capital, seeing above him the mighty walls, the pinnacles and palaces, the hanging gardens rising in tiers above the city, seeing before him the processional way paved with coloured tiles, that led through the triumphal gateway of Ishtar to Nebuchadnezzar's palace glittering in the sun. . . .

Persepolis . . . is pure ruin and legend. The very name has a rich, magical, incantatory sound, suggesting Persian pleasures, palaces, pillars, playing fountains, pealing bells, dancing girls, luscious gardens of ripe pears, apples, plums, persimmons, and purling waters. Christopher Marlowe, haunted by it, made it the centre of Tamburlaine's martial dreams, though in Tamburlaine's day the ancient Achaemenid capital was a ruinous, almost abandoned city of no account. Unhampered by this, the Persian lord speaks to the Persian king of 'your merchants of Persepolis', who trade with western lands, and Tamburlaine breaks into wishful thinking:

> Is it not passing brave to be a king
> And ride in triumph through Persepolis?

'O my Lord,' his follower agrees, ''tis sweet and full of pomp.' And so, indeed, kings had found it, during the centuries from its building by Cyrus, Darius and Xerxes to its eclipse as Takht-i-Jamshid (for the Persians would have it that the huge palaces had been built by Jamshid, who in them gloried and drank deep). But in 322 Alexander and his Macedonian army, chasing the Persians over the pass, rode down into the great valley a-lust for the fabulous city where the Persians stored prodigious treasure. In the palace halls on the great terrace they feasted with their courtesans, and then, so the tradition ran,

> Alexander, Thais, and the Macedonian soldiers,
> Reeling with their torches through the Persian palaces
> Wrecked to flaring fragments pillared Persepolis. . . .

by way of vengeance for Athens. Alexander's 'frolic at Persepolis', John Evelyn tolerantly called it; the French traveller, Chardin, more sharply, '*sa brutale débauche, par où il commença de brûler Persépolis.'* But this legend, put about by Greek and Roman historians, is no longer so well thought of; even Chardin doubted it. There are traces of fire; but the wreck of Persepolis, the throwing down of so many hundreds of columns, so many halls and sculptures, could scarcely have been Alexander's work. Earthquake, time, enemy attacks, the vandalism and neglect of the Arabs, worked together on Persepolis which seems, by the end of the tenth century, to have been pretty well a ruin. A ruin always famous in legend, and always a sight for tourists, who described and drew its buildings from the Middle Ages down to today. 'Those famous ruins called Chihil Minar, of the forty columns, the illustrious remains of the ancient Persepolis, which I so ardently and so long had wished to see,' della Valle wrote. . . .

Sir Thomas Herbert, in 1628, admired it even more.

'Let us now (what pace you please) to Persepolis, not much out of the road: but were it a thousand times further, it merits our paines to view it; being indeed the only brave Antique-Monument (not in Persia alone) but through all the Orient. . . . A Citie so excellent that Quintus Curtius and Diodorus Siculus intitle it the richest and most lovely Citie under the sunne.'

He describes it as it had once been: the triple wall, of delicate polished marble entered by burnished gates; the temple of Diana, of rich marble and porphyry and refined gold ('a bait Antiochus the avaricious Atheist long had nibbled at, but could not swallow it'); the royal Palace, cut out of the marble rock, with roof and casements of gold, silver, amber and ivory; inside it gold and glittering gems; in one room a vine presented by Pythias, the stalk pure gold, the grapes, pearls and carbuncles; the treasure everywhere fabulous, and the Macedonian spoiler must have carried away many millions, on three thousand mules. . . .

Astonishing, unbelievable, the greatness of the Persians; it is this fantastic, incredible past that haloes what Herbert calls the 'ribs and ruins' on their high platform, so that it is less these that are seen and enjoyed than 'the old Persian magnificence' that haunts them. Indeed the pleasure of Persepolis is more a pleasure of ideas and imagination than of actual visual delight. Here are the courts (or so the silly inhabitants say) where Jamshid gloried and drank deep; the lizard still keeps them, but the lion, shy of archaeologists, has retired. But, anyhow, here was Elam, here was Persia. Here were the palace halls, with their cedar and silver roofs, their coloured hangings fastened by silver rings to pillars of marble, their mosaic pavements, their great blocks of richly carved stone; here reigned Darius; here the Macedonian victor feasted, Thais at his side; here the ghosts of slain Greeks cried vengeance, tossing their torches as they routed through the banquet hall, till

> *The king seized a flambeau with zeal to destroy,*
> *Thais led the way,*
> *To light him to his prey,*
> *And, like another Helen, fired another Troy.*

Yet students of architecture as well as of history and legend have found rich rewards in the study of what Thais and all the later destroyers have left. For the last two centuries they have poured forth praises and drawings in volumes comparable in size with the huge ruinated palaces beneath the mountain-side. Of all the reminders of past greatness in Iran, said the admirable Dieulafoys in 1887, not one had impressed them more vividly than these skeletons of palaces. Architects are gratified by the findings of new elements in the Achaemenid style - Pharaonic Egyptian, Chaldaeo-Assyrian, Ionic Greek. The ruins are a rich medley; reliefs, friezes and capitals suggesting Assyria surmount Graeco–Egyptian pillars – 'the columns of the Nile on the plains of Persia'. There are unattractive, un-Persian monsters, half-man, half-beast. The decoration is at once rich and formal; the polished dark grey stone gives it a grave air; the pillars of Persepolis have not the golden grace of Palmyra, the deep orange glow of Baalbek, the changing rainbow hues of Petra. And they have the air, from a distance, of an unusually fine row of ninepins. The general effect of the great rocky terraces with the grey roofless colonnade, backed by the mountain-side honeycombed with tombs, and approached by the great double flight of shallow stairs, so suitable for horses, has been thought by some travellers just a little short of superb. . . .

Sir Robert Ker Porter, in 1821, had the pleasure of riding the stairs. 'I invariably rode my horse up and down them during my visits to their interesting summit.' Of the buildings on the interesting summit he made admirable drawings and descriptions; previous travellers he found inaccurate. Nor did he approve the vulgar way in which they had inscribed their names on the polished walls of the great portal. Easily corrupted, however, he would appear to have done the same himself; Dr Ainsworth, surgeon and geologist of the Euphrates expedition of 1836, found his name carved, together with those of Pietro della Valle, Niebuhr, Chardin, Rich, and many others, on a wall; this self-recording is, indeed, one of the last infirmities of noble, as of baser, minds. . . .

Now that we can identify everything, now that the

site has been explored and labelled, it has inevitably lost some of its romance. Robert Byron, for instance, was annoyed and disillusioned; Persepolis was in the hands of the German excavators.

'In the old days [he complained], you rode up the steps on to the platform. You made a camp there, while the columns and winged beasts kept their solitude beneath the stars, and not a sound or a movement disturbed the empty moonlit plain. You thought of Darius and Alexander. You were alone with the ancient world. You saw Asia as the Greeks saw it, and you felt their magic breath stretching out towards China itself. . . . Today you step out of a motor, while a couple of lorries thunder by in a cloud of dust. You find the approaches guarded by walls. You enter by leave of a porter, and are greeted on reaching the platform by a light railway, a neo-German hostel, and a code of academic malice compiled from Chicago. These useful additions clarify the intelligence. You may persuade yourself, in spite of them, into a mood of romance. But the mood they invite is that of a critic at an exhibition. That is the penalty of greater knowledge.'

It is the familiar tragedy of archaeology – the sacrifice of beauty to knowledge. Burckhardt wept over it on revisiting the de-mossed Greek temples of Sicily after twenty years; Augustus Hare over Hadrian's cleaned-up villa; we today over all the excavated, tidied-up monuments of the world. Robert Byron, looking on Persepolis, was put out of conceit

with it altogether. He found the columns surprising but meaningless, the stairs only fine because so many of them, the terrace of buildings impressive because so massive, the crenellations on the parapet ugly, the cold, shining grey stone repellent and like an aluminium saucepan. It is possible not to be transported by Persepolis; perhaps, to approach it in the right mood, one needs a horse to ride up the stairs; motor-cars take them less well. It was after scaling the great stairway on his sixteen-hand steed that Colonel P. M. Sykes, in 1914, was overwhelmed with admiration of what he saw at the top.

But some recent travellers have found the old Persian magnificence still haunting the column-strewn terrace like a ghost. 'Xerxes and Darius haunted us that evening,' one of these wrote. He saw in the moonlight, among the litter of broken pillars,

'the invisible causeways, staircases and triumphal processions of men in gold armour, royal bed-chambers and the golden throne, all lost and gathered in the dust. . . . You heard music. . . .'

It was, this traveller remarked, like being drunk, to see all this ruinous beauty under the moon. Pacing the reconstructed harem, a young Persian archaeologist recalled the glorious Achaemenian past, while in the deep ditches the excavators dug for what more of this past they might find.

But, at Persepolis, the ghosts of lost splendour are better than anything dug from the earth.

Persepolis, Iran. Relief from the mausoleum of Darius III

33 Nineveh, Iraq. Detail of a man-headed beast
The broken head of one of the strange stone creatures which stood at the gates of the Assyrian palaces at Nineveh and Khorsabad. Later copied at Persepolis, they had the body and legs of a lion or a bull, the wings of an eagle and the bearded head of a man, with an elaborate head-piece of formalized horns and feathered crown. Carved as symbols of strength—to protect the king against evil—some of them were twice as tall as a man. They date from the height of Assyrian power, and were the work of the sculptors of Sargon II at Khorsabad and of his son Sennacherib at Nineveh, in the eighth century BC.

34–5 Nineveh, Iraq. Frieze showing King Assurbanipal in his chariot
The glory of the king and the might of his armies is depicted in stone by the sculptors of Nineveh. It is a state occasion: the king stands in his decorated chariot with driver and an attendant who holds a tasselled awning; in his left hand is the symbolic bow, his right hand is raised in the formal salute of the time. The two horses (the second assumed by the sculptor to be precisely hidden except at the head) are decked in a king's trappings, their tails elaborately groomed; before them stand the royal guards and the whole scene is posed on the banks of the Tigris, represented below. It is a celebration of victory, for the beaten enemy lies symbolically beneath the horses' feet.

36 Persepolis, Iran. Armenian tribute bearers
Led by a Persian guard, Armenians bring tribute—a horse and (out of the picture) a vase of precious metal—to the 'King of Kings'. The Achaemenid kings of Persia ruled over the first great empire of recorded history, which stretched from India to Egypt. Its centre was the ancient site of Persepolis, and it was here, on a gigantic stage measuring 1650 by 980 feet, that Darius I, his son Xerxes I and grandson Artaxerxes I built their palaces and stored their treasure. The empire reached its greatest glory in the fifth century BC. Then, in 330 BC, its power was destroyed by Alexander the Great.
Persepolis was built to record and maintain the power of a dynasty. The Persian and Median nobles who came to the celebrations on New Year's Day entered a noble gateway, with wide stairs 'suitable for horses', and were led through the north entrance of the Apadana or audience hall and out by the stairway on the east. There they could view in magnificent bas-relief a procession of twenty-three subject nations, with court nobles, Persians and Medes, their horses and royal chariots and ranks of Susian guards. As they descended the steps they passed the detail in this photograph, the first of a long centre register depicting tribute bearers. The tree motif is a stylized pine (*Pinus prutia*), copied from the trees which Darius I planted on the vast esplanade to which the stairway led.

37 Persepolis, Iran. A fallen bull's-head capital
Today the tumbled columns of Persepolis rest in the dust and here and there one of the elaborate twin animal capitals—like this bull's head with starting eyes—lies broken, breathing immortal indignation at majesty outraged.

38 Persepolis, Iran. A Susian warrior
A guard from Susa stands immobile, his lance held erect. Long ranks of such warriors, identically carved, stand on the frieze of the eastern staircase of the Apadana.

39 Persepolis, Iran. Lion seizing bull
In front of the east staircase of the Apadana, at each end of the frieze, and repeated elsewhere in the palaces, appear replicas of this powerful lion, strength rippling from its muscles, its claws and teeth digging deep into the hindquarters of a rearing bull. Showing Assyrian influence, and brutal to modern eyes, the struggle is said to have symbolized the triumph of good over evil.

40–1 Persepolis, Iran. The Apadana
Of the Apadana, or Audience Hall, itself, there stand today only thirteen tall columns. Pietro della Valle in 1621 counted twenty-five columns erect. The original number was seventy-two. On three sides, twelve columns each formed stately porticoes, the central area, with thirty-six, was nearly 200 feet square and could, it is estimated, accommodate 10,000 people. The columns were topped by stable and highly decorative capitals of a kind found nowhere in the West. On the fluted shafts rest the foreparts of two animals, back to back, bulls, griffins or human-headed bulls. Cedarwood beams, crossed to support the terraced roof, rested on the animals' backs and between their horns.
The view in the picture at left looks across the raised floor. The picture at right was taken looking upwards from the eastern staircase. Below the floor Darius placed two stone boxes, each containing two foundation plaques, one in gold, the other in silver. The text engraved on them in Old Persian, Elamite and Babylonian reads: 'Darius, the Great King, King of Kings, King of the Countries, son of Hystaspes, the Achaemenid. Saith Darius the King: This is the kingdom which I possess from the land of the Sakas on this side of Sogdiana as far as Kush, from India to Sardis. Over this Ahuramazda has granted me dominion, he who is great above all Gods. May Ahuramazda protect me and my Royal House.'

42 Persepolis, Iran. A Median usher before Darius
The relief figure of a Mede (in shadow) reports deferentially to the king, while behind him (in the light) stand two bearded Persians, one carrying a spear, the other a scent-box. It has been suggested that the draperies of the Persepolis reliefs, formalized still but flowing more freely than their Assyrian counterparts, could have been the work of Ionian Greeks.
The scene is a detail from one of two identical bas-reliefs, 20 feet long; they were found in a porticoed courtyard before a hall with ninety-nine columns in the centre of the Treasury, which had expanded, as tribute poured in from the subject peoples, over the whole of the south-east corner of Persepolis. When Alexander captured the palaces in 330 BC

it required, according to the historian Diodorus Siculus, '3000 camels and innumerable mules from Susa, to carry away the treasures'.

43 Babylon, Iraq. Walls of the Ishtar Gate

The lower walls of the approach to the main gate to the inner city of Babylon carry the same decorations as the gate itself—alternating tiers of dragons and bulls, attributes of the ancient gods, Marduk and Adad. Standing out against a background tinted blue with lapis lazuli, the dragons were white, their horns, forked tongues and claws picked out in yellow, the bulls were dark brown, with horns and hoofs green, hide and tail-tips blue. The Babylonians themselves covered these walls, which archaeologists have since dug out, to raise the level of road and gate.

Almost all the surviving ruins at Babylon belong to the city known as New Babylon, built in the seventh century BC by Nabopolassar and his son Nebuchadnezzar after the Assyrian Sennacherib had diverted the Euphrates to destroy the old city. But the power which defeated Nineveh had vanished and the splendour had begun to fade when the city was conquered by Cyrus the Persian in 539 BC and after him by Darius and Xerxes. By the beginning of the Christian era all the grim Biblical prophecies had been fulfilled—the fine city which Herodotus saw was a heap of débris in the desert. (See also p. 238)

PERSEPOLIS

a   Stairway to the Terrace
b   Gate-House of Xerxes (the 'Gate of All Countries')
c   Processional Way
d   North Stairway of the Apadana
e   The Apadana (Audience Hall)
f   East Stairway of the Apadana
g   Tripylon
h   Palace of Darius I (Banquet Hall)
j   Palace of Xerxes (Banquet Hall)
k   Throne Hall of One Hundred Columns
m   Unfinished Gate-House
n, o, p   Military Area
q   Royal Treasury, Hall of One Hundred Columns
r   Royal Treasury, Hall of Ninety-Nine Columns (temporary Throne Hall built by Darius I)
s   Storerooms of the Royal Treasury
t   South Façade of the Terrace, overlooking the plain (the Royal Box is in the centre)
u   Direction of Mausoleum of Darius III
▲   Ceremonial route for Persian and Median notables
△   Ceremonial route for visiting delegations

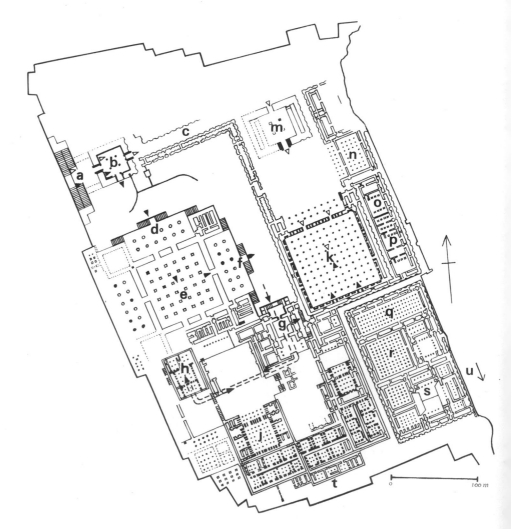

33

THE RUINOUS PARADISE

Syria, Mesopotamia, all the far spaces of Arabia, from the Turkish frontier southward to Palestine and Transjordan, from the Lebanon eastward to the Euphrates and across it, are the ruinous paradise of archaeologists and romantics (the former class are always the latter, the latter but rarely the former). . . . Ruined Ptolemaic, Roman and Byzantine cities, or isolated fragments of temples, arches, columns, paved streets, are strewn about the desert as milestones or sheepfolds are in lands of less high pedigree. Entering some Arab village of squalid hovels, we are in a Roman colony, among temple columns, triumphal arches, traces of theatres and baths which no one has had the intellect or the cleanliness to use since the Arabs expelled the civilized Graeco-Roman-Syrian inhabitants and squatted among their broken monuments, stabling their horses in the nave of a Christian basilica, their camels in a richly carved pagan temple, their families in mud huts clustering about the proscenium of a theatre: the broken heirlooms of the race that ruled stand like desolate ghosts among the squalor. Or they stand alone, lonely outposts in the desert, with perhaps a Syrian herdsman and his lean flock lying in the shade of what was, a millennium and a half ago, a marble colonnade. This shade, those fallen capitals for seats, those broken shafts for tethering, this enigmatic but familiar suggestion of a mansion in the desert spaces, may be all the ruin-pleasure the oblivious herdsman gets; unless some travelling enthusiast chances by, and . . . starts measuring each pillar and surmising past magnificence from the broken stones. Familiar, perhaps, from hearsay or experience, with the strange ways of Franks (who have always pretended this unaccountable interest in ruins, but in reality, as all Arabs know, are looking for treasure) the herdsman may reap an immediate reward for civility and officiousness, or, when the inquisitive Frank is off the scenes, he may do a little groping and digging himself about the sand-drifts that hold those fallen temples and arches; for a while the pleasures of brief hope may be his. No more ruin-excitement than this, we believe; unless that of quarrying away the ancient stones for houses and folds. But there is no being sure that, throughout the long centuries of apathy and destruction and greed, there has not been a haunting awareness of the stone signatures of those extraordinary, unknown, mysterious races who once dominated and held the desert, building in it an alien culture, setting it about with alien fortresses and gods, leaving it with the débris of a whole civilization strewn about its face. . . .

Improbable glamour is . . . the apt description of Petra, that strange, lovely and most famous dead city carved out of the rock cliffs of Arabia. Unlike most famous ruins, Petra has not had a long and unbroken stream of foreign visitors. Since Saladin drove the crusaders out of Palestine, there is no certainly identifiable account of Petra by any European traveller until J. L. Burckhardt, got up as an Arab Sheik, explored the desert in 1812, and thought it 'very probable that the ruins in Wadi Musa are those of the ancient Petra'. Arabia Petraea was not a tempting land to travel: 'Countries which are little known and but thinly inhabited,' Karsten Niebuhr described it in 1762, 'the inhabitants of which wander among dry sands and rocks, seeking here and there a few spots which afford some scanty food for their cattle. None but Bedouins haunt these deserts.' Since Burckhardt, they have been haunted by a stream of explorers eager and intelligent and extremely courageous in the face of the apparently excessively alarming habits of the residents in and near the ancient Nabataean capital, who used to evince the strongest xenophobia against visitors. Burckhardt, having apprehended quickly that, though every prospect pleased, man was pretty vile, only spent there the inside of a day, his excitement over the wonders he had discovered giving way to prudence. . . .

Burckhardt's description of what he saw was astonishingly brilliant. He approached Petra, as nearly all subsequent travellers have done, along the deep gorge of the Sik, where rock walls tower overhead, shutting the ravine into intimidating gloom. . . . This romantic gorge is by now familiar to us; all travellers have described its incidents – the ruined arch (now unfortunately disappeared) spanning the ravine near its beginning, a fit entry to so noble a capital city, the sudden apparition, more than a mile farther on, of a deep red façade ninety feet high, with pillars, statues, bas-reliefs – the two-storeyed temple of Isis, called by the Arabs El-Kazneh, or the Treasure of Pharaoh . . . and then . . . the Roman theatre, of the first century A D, a semi-circle of thirty-three tiers of seats hewn out of the rocky side of a mountain and surrounded by tombs far older than the theatre; some of them climb up from the top row of seats. 'Strange contrast!' . . . wrote Dr Edward Robinson in 1838 . . . 'where a taste for the frivolities of the day was at the same time gratified by the magnificence of the tombs; amusement in a cemetery; a theatre in the midst of sepulchres.'

Beyond the theatre begins the town, Roman in period, lying on both banks of the Wadi Musa in a large irregular oblong. It was a fine populous city; the remains of buildings, public and private, are thick on the ground, covering about two miles; there are three market places, a forum, baths, gymnasia, shops, colonnades, private houses, all lying in this rock-guarded valley, whose mountain walls rival any flower garden in rich tints and shades; they have been compared to rainbows, and to the shifting hues of watered silk; though sandstone red is the prevailing tone, the 'rose-red city half as old as time' of a very bad Newdigate poem is inaccurate both visually and mathematically. . . .

A great three-bayed gate gives access to a way still partly paved, leading to the city, of which the centre is an immense market place, with shops and galleries opening out of it. Here the caravans of merchants from east and west brought and sold their wares; it is a strange and ghostly scene, whispering with the echoes of chaffering Nabataean merchants two thousand years ago: up from southern Arabia they came, with their camel trains, their rich bales, their spices, ivory and amber, calling *en route* at Petra, crowding in the market places of the rock city, looked down on by steep rainbow heights wherein were carved something like a thousand sepulchres. . . .

The heyday of Petra was in the first and second centuries AD, after annexation by Rome had turned Arabia Petraea and the old Nabataean kingdom into a Roman province. It was under Trajan and Hadrian and Alexander Severus that Petra assumed its Hellenistic–Roman air; the theatre was hewn in the mountain-side, the city filled with substantial Roman splendour, the cliffs with Roman tombs. The development of the style in tombs can be traced; early to later Nabataean; then Graeco-Roman, with still the oriental touch; sumptuousness growing steadily, until some time in the third century, when Palmyra stole Petra's caravan trade and the Persian empire engulfed its glory. A century later, it had dwindled to an unprosperous little town, a Christian bishopric until the Saracen conquest; the crusaders held it for a time in the twelfth century, and built on the top of a mountain south of the city a fine castle. After Saladin had swept them out of it, there is little more news of Petra until Burckhardt found it. Since then it has become news indeed, and the Mecca of romantic eastern travellers, for if ever a dead city held romance it is Petra. Wild, Arab-infested, hewn out of ruddy rock in the midst of a mountain wilderness, sumptuous in ornament and savage in environs, poised in wildness like a great carved opal glowing in a desert, this lost caravan city of Edom staggers the most experienced traveller. Even Sir Henry Layard, robbed and enraged by villainous Arabs in 1840, and taking a poor view of the architecture, which he found debased, of a bad period and corrupt style, and wanting both in elegance and grandeur, admitted that these ruins were unlike any other ancient city in the world. As to Captains Irby and Mangles . . . they were overcome with enthusiasm for Petra, when they visited it in 1818, oddly dressed as Bedouins (for dressing up as Bedouins used to be, perhaps is still, among the pleasures of visiting Arab ruins). The awful sublimity of the approach ('Salvator Rosa never conceived so savage and suitable a quarter for Banditti'), the riches of the decoration contrasting with the wild scenery, the summits of the rocks presenting 'nature in her most savage and romantic form, while their bases are worked out in all the symmetry of art', the whole hewn out of the living, glowing rock. . . . It all made a most singular scene, wherein they dared spend only two days for fear of the residents. . . . Léon de Laborde, ten years later, spent eight days, and wrote a detailed description with drawings: over his precision enthusiasm hovers like a winged spirit; he had never seen anything so remarkable and romantic, and nor, he persuades us, have we. He added to his pleasures by extensive quoting from the Bible, for this is what the earlier visitors to Petra loved to do, reiterating the curses on Edom. *O thou that dwellest in the clefts of the rock, that holdest the height of the hill, though thou shouldst make thy nest as high as the eagle, I will bring thee down from thence, saith the Lord. Also, Edom shall be a desolation; everyone that goeth by shall be astonished.* Everyone, in fact, is; whether, like Burckhardt and Layard, they spend only a day in the city in the clefts of the rock, or . . . whether they stay long enough to draw the monuments and examine all the tombs and make the steep ascent to the monastery of El Deir on its mountain. Drunk with colour, beauty, strangeness, and all the peculiar excitement imparted by antiquity, they have sometimes ended a perfect day by supping and sleeping in one of the better tombs. This is what Mr Bartlett did, in the 1840s, when he, surrounded by a posse of Arabs, visited Petra in the course of writing his book, *Forty Days in the Desert*. . . .

Such are the pleasures afforded by Petra, 'that extraordinary rock-hewn capital of Edom, which, by its singular wildness, even yet seems, beyond any other place, to thrill the imagination and waken the love of adventure. . . .'

It is ruined Greece and Rome which occupy Syria. The dead Byzantine cities, the dead outposts of Rome, these lie crumbling on mountain, desert and plain, lost in time and in the oblivion of barbarians, but invincibly in occupation. . . . 'This kingdom,' wrote William Lithgow, mooning about Syria in 1612, 'this kingdom hath suffered many alterations especially by the Persians, Grecians, Armenians, Romans, Egyptians, lastly by the Turks, and daily molested by the incursive Arabs.' The incursive Arabs, now in possession, have not had the energy or the means to build their own world upon the ruins of the old; they accept the dead cities as nothing strange, the dead cities of Greece, Seleucia, Rome and Byzantium, brooding like ghosts over desert and mountain and fertile valley, from Antioch and Aleppo in the north to Wadi Araba in the far south, while among them the great crusaders' castles ride the desert like moored battleships. . . .

'The ruins of the Roman past remain, preserved to some extent by the very depopulation and misery of the centuries that have intervened. Had an organized civilization been maintained in these hills, the mark of Rome would have been overlaid. No such civilization lingered on, and for over a decaying millennium the ancient buildings have crumbled uncomprehended. . . . Rome rises among hovels, and the ancient sites are honeycombed with the shapeless structures of the peasantry. It is a strange irony to find baths and theatres in such a country, or triumphal avenues down which only a flock of ragged goats are driven out and back at dawn and sunset.'

This was written particularly of the Jebel country, where Roman cities, baths, markets and theatres stick strangely out of the rocky basalt wilderness: Chahba, which became Philippopolis after the emperor Philip who was born there; Kanawat, full of ruined streets, Roman temples, Byzantine churches, vaulted cisterns; Bosra, once the capital of Roman Arabia, succeeding Petra, preceding Palmyra, as the most important of the caravan trade cities of the desert. Bosra is today one of the happiest of the ruin-hunters' Syrian haunts; it has everything.

'Bosrah stood up, black and imposing, before us for miles before we arrived, a mass of columns and triumphal arches with the castle dominating the whole. I went up the square tower of the minaret and looked out over the town – columns and black square

towers over every ruined church and mosque, and the big castle, and the countless masses of fallen stone. I had been joined by a cheerful, handsome person, the Mamur . . . who climbed with me in and out of the little churches and the fallen walls and the ruined houses. Such a spectacle of past magnificence and present squalor it would be difficult to conceive. There were inscriptions everywhere, Latin, Greek, Cufic and Arabic, built into the walls of the Fellahin houses, topsy turvy, together with the perforated slabs that were once windows, and bits of columns and capitals of pillars. . . . At last he took me to the top of the castle and introduced me to the head of the soldiers, who produced chairs and coffee on his rooftop, and subsequently glasses of arack and water in his room below.'

Such are the amenities: coffee on roof-tops, views of the great jumble of medieval ruin, arack and water with cheerful handsome Mamurs, the general sense of magnificence. Behind these the ghosts of Roman legions stalk Trajan's streets between ghostly columns; a Roman triumphal arch still stands; ruins of temples, colonnades, baths, lie about. Somewhere there sits the ghost of the Prophet who was to overturn the east, studying Christian theology. . . .

One of the most showy and exciting ruin-pleasures in the world, has, for several centuries, been Palmyra, that ancient Arab settlement in the Syrian desert. City of legend more dubious and remote than some, it has lost a few centuries of age and prestige since it began to be suspected not, after all, to be that Tadmor which King Solomon built in the wilderness, but to have grown from an Arab caravan halt on an oasis to become later a trading settlement on the merchant route across the desert from sea to sea. After the decline of Petra in A D 105 it largely took Petra's place; the merchant caravans went that way, carrying their silks and spices, ivory, ebony and gems, to the rich Arab desert city, which was to grow under the empire into such political importance, such dazzling grace.

What we see today, the fabulous golden-ochre colonnades, the Temple of the Sun with its pillared court, the great field of ruins like a garden of broken daffodils lying within the long low shattered line of Justinian's wall, is Syrian Graeco-Roman of the more florid period, and has excited, perhaps, a more startled ecstasy in beholders than almost any other of the world's wrecked cities.

Even the Arabs of early centuries made poems about it when it passed into their possession; and to the medieval Jews who made their homes there it seemed of palatial magnificence. . . .

It was the Aleppo merchants' account in the Philosophical Transactions of the Royal Society that put Palmyra on the map as a goal for British travellers; ever since, it has been the marvel and admiration of all who could get so far, gleaming like a desert mirage before dazzled western eyes. . . . Fabulous city, its prestige heightened by its difficulty of access, by lying in the middle of a vast intractable desert, a very long way from anywhere else. To reach it was a job, entailing a great fuss of camels, dromedaries, tents and escorts – all the expensive paraphernalia of desert expeditions. Those who made it usually had some high intention, such as counting and measuring the columns, making drawings and plans, copying inscriptions, stealing a few carvings and sculptures, or meditating on the ruins of greatness and composing a book. Yet they all found many pleasures on the way, even apart from the breathless delight of beholding what they held to be the first and most extensive ruins in the world. . . .

The approach evocative has been very usual at Palmyra. Particularly is Zenobia evoked: Volney had a long conversation with her spirit as he meditated there in 1792, composing his work on the Ruins of Empire. The more scholarly and less fanciful Dr Wood and Dr Dawkins, in 1738, thought less about Zenobia and ruined empires than about the ruins themselves. . . . The intellectual stimulus of ruins is perhaps a theme worth pursuing; it must be accepted, anyhow, as a fact. *'Je vous salue, ruines solitaires,'* Volney apostrophized them. . . .

Not so soberly did Lady Hester Stanhope – 'that highly eccentric gentlewoman', as Kinglake called her – take her Palmyrene pleasures, when, against all advice, she rode into the desert city on a white Arab horse in 1813, accompanied by Mr Bruce, the faithful Dr Meryon, and her Arab suite. . . . After resting for a day, she mounted her horse and rode about the ruins, tiring out the elderly sheik who accompanied her on foot, examining everything. . . . In the evenings there were revels in the open space in the temple ruins, coffee-drinking, story-telling and dancing. Lady Hester's name was cut in a conspicuous place as a memorial. She had never reached before, she was never to reach again, these dizzy heights of glory, when Zenobia's capital acclaimed her as its queen. One may say that no one has ever enjoyed himself or herself more in any ruins than did Pitt's niece in Palmyra; it was *Ruinenlust* in its highest, its most regal degree. . . .

Jerash, Gerasa, that once great city of the Decapolis, now one of the most beautiful columned ruins anywhere, had a briefer heyday than Bosra, but more greatness, more brilliant a prosperity, and has left far more to show for it. Lying in a remote valley among the mountains of Gilead, with the small river Chrysorrhoas running through it, it was once called Antioch, which suggests a Seleucid origin of the second century BC; but there are earlier attributions, notably to Ptolemy II, who changed Amman into the Hellenistic Philadelphia in the third century, and even to Alexander the Great. It is supposed that each of these and general prosperity may have helped in 'the emergence of Jerash from the chrysalis village of mud huts to the brightly coloured butterfly of an Hellenistic town'. But most of the buildings we see now date from the magnificent Roman rebuilding of the first and second centuries AD. . . .

Approaching Jerash by the rough road from the south, one sees the triple triumphal arch ahead, its columns acanthus-based; beyond it the south gate, the colonnaded oval of the forum lying within it, and from there the paved main street drives straight across the city to the north gate, deeply rutted with the wheels of chariots. Drive cautiously along it in a car or jeep; you will pass on your left the glories of Roman Jerash, the cathedral with its second-century façade and its great flights of steps, and the majestic Temple of Artemis behind it. By the edge of the street is the deliciously decadent, conch-decorated nymphaeum, with a sprawl of little Arabs in the fountain basin. Excavated Byzantine churches group east and west among the baths. To the right, across the wooded river, there are more baths, more churches, a mosque, and the mud-built, flat-roofed Circassian village.

You pass excavators at their work, with pick-axe and spade, while others haul up great blocks or capitals into position, and set prostrate pillars on end, for reconstruction proceeds; we may have in the end a Gerasa of the second and third centuries, and very beautiful it will look. Somewhat shaken by Gerasa's paved street, you arrive at the archaeologist's house, and, from the cool shade of its terrace, have a magnificent view over the tawny, columned city, whose wall was two miles round. Here once was luxury, culture, drama, amusement, gladiatorial sport, flourishing commerce, religion, all the amenities of a prosperous Roman colony: the sheer beauty of that well-appointed, seemly city lying above the oleandrous-banked river breathes like a memory about its broken ruins. Destruction, step by step, slew it. The Byzantine Christians built their churches from the pagan shrines; the Persians invaded it in 614, the Arabs in 635, earthquakes shook it, eighth-century caliphs destroyed images and mosaic floors; by the twelfth century it had been long abandoned, and the Artemis temple was turned into a fortress, captured by crusaders, and burnt down. The city became a ruin-field. 'To this day Arabs as far afield as south Palestine, when they wish to speak of something as extremely ruinous, say: "It is like the ruins of Jerash".' Yet, surveyed from the terrace above it, the colonnaded, paved, templed and fountained town, grass-grown and shrubbed but laid out in streets with tetrapylons and the remains of arcaded shops, and set about with graceful shattered buildings, does not wear an air of desolation. These courts, these steps that climb up to noble Christian and pagan shrines, these baths and play-houses, those columns rising up as from a long sleep, the whole set in the green solitude of the circling ruin-sprouting hills; this fragment of Rome in the wilderness has a lovely civility. More of it is emerging month by month, more going up; even the mud village which has during the past century lain at its gates and expedited its ruin, cannot spoil this beauty. . . .

The position, the mellow golden colour of the huge stones, the towering citadel of pillared buildings, seen for miles along the valley of approach, the size and magnificence which has sustained, though with damage, the assaults of Man and Nature down the ages, the stagey splendour of the whole, make Baalbek unique. Wood, who saw and described it before the earthquakes of 1759 further devastated it, called it 'the remains of the boldest plans we ever saw attempted in architecture'. Seeing it as a superb work of art, spectators have discussed whether sunset or moonlight is the more rewarding hour in which to gaze on it. Many discriminating admirers have upheld the moonlight view. . . .

Baalbek . . . had always been visited and admired by travellers, long before it became a tourist resort with a railway station and hotels. Lying on the Aleppo–Damascus route, it was popular with both merchants and pilgrims. Its origins are lost in the mists of Phoenician antiquity; its great Graeco-Roman temples stand on the sites of temples to older gods than Jupiter, Venus or Mercury. The richly decorated oriental late-Roman architecture is that of Palmyra; the colour a deeper gold, like that of marmalade or amber honey. The Greeks and Romans called it Heliopolis, the city of the sun; it became a magnificently decorated Roman colony. In the second century Antoninus Pius built the Temple of Jupiter

(probably to replace a temple of Baal) 'which', said a seventh-century writer, 'was one of the wonders of the world', as indeed its ruin is today. . . .

The pleasures enjoyed by visitors to Baalbek have always had a particular note of rapture. Lamartine, though a little confused, was overcome with delight. . . . A good time, too, was had by the diligent antiquarian traveller, Dr Richard Pococke, in the 1740s. . . . The Pasha treated him with the utmost politeness, conversed about world affairs, asked him who was the greatest prince in Europe, and showed him a young tiger. The pleasure of Baalbek to the redoubtable Lady Hester Stanhope was not quite so heady as that which she had savoured at Palmyra. It was cold, as everyone, except during the hot summer months, finds Baalbek; the first snows had fallen. Lady Hester and her suite pitched their tents a short way out of the town, in the ruins of an old mosque, in a valley full of springs that bubbled into stone basins (probably Ras-el-Ain). A shady path led through woods to the town. In the distance towered the snow-topped peaks of Lebanon; above the encircling gardens rose the acropolis and the six columns of the great temple. Dr Meryon, when they visited the great temple, took a piece of charcoal and wrote on the wall of the inner temple, which was covered with names, a Latin quatrain in his employer's praise, which ended '*Esther, si pereant marmora, semper erit.*' But Lady Hester (a gentlewoman, even if eccentric) made him rub it out. In spite of the weather, they spent a week at Baalbek. . . .

That particular romantic pleasure, when the city was a jumble of unsorted ruins, and travellers pitched their tents in the court of the great temple, has faded since Baalbek became a fashionable modern Levantine town. But the acropolis remains, with its orange-hued temples, pillars, courts, basilica, and fallen columns; and the excavations of the last fifty years have revealed buildings more clearly. These, with the towered Arab walls and great ruined mosque, should be, for most travellers, enough; though the scholarly Dr Wood found a moment between his plans and descriptions to regret that the ancient female beauty and kindness for which Baalbek was once famous seemed to have vanished altogether. He noted that the Arab inhabitants took pleasure in speaking of the 'hours of dalliance' which King Solomon, they said, had enjoyed in Baalbek; 'a subject on which the warm imagination of the Arabs is apt to be too particular.'

51 Baalbek, Lebanon. Temple of Bacchus

The smaller of the two temples at Baalbek, the Temple of Bacchus, is larger than the Parthenon. It is a masterpiece of later classical architecture. The outer wall and broken columns of the peristyle, one side of which is shown in this photograph, glow golden brown in the evening sun.

Baalbek, 'City of the Sun', was described by Robert Wood as 'the remains of the boldest plans we ever saw attempted in architecture'. Its temple complex stands high above the plain between the two Lebanons, raised on a huge substructure containing some of the largest single blocks of stone in the world. Grandiose, ornate by classical standards, the richest Corinthian buildings of the Roman world, Baalbek's ruins still bear witness to the security and prosperity the Romans brought to the edge of the Asian desert.

52–3 Petra, Jordan. Nabataean tombs behind the Roman theatre

A semicircle of thirty-three tiers of seats was cut into the rainbow-coloured rock-face of Petra by the Romans, and destroyed many of the earlier tombs behind. The actors could play to a large living audience, but rarely can entertainment have been presented in the presence of so grim a gallery, staring with the empty eyes of death. The small tombs are typical: a simple house front with a slight backward slope and a single doorway with two sides converging.

Petra, 'the Rock', lies within a high sandstone outcrop in southern Jordan, a desert area which was part of the ancient kingdom of Edom. It is approached, on horseback, from Ain Musa, 'Moses Spring'. The bed of the Wadi Musa leads through the famous Sik, the gorge at times only 5 feet wide with bulging sides 300 feet high, cut by the water in the soft rock. Paved by the Romans, with separate tunnels to carry the water, it can now be dangerous when the rare floods sweep down.

When the Edomites left Petra, in 588 BC, the nomad Nabataeans took their place. Luxuries from the Far and Middle East, silks and spices, pearls and precious woods reached the Red Sea port of Akaba; myrrh and frankincense from the Queen of Sheba's country, ivory, apes and black slaves from Africa came by caravan up the Red Sea coast — and Petra, on the route north to Damascus, to the Mediterranean coast for trade bound for Greece and Rome and to Gaza for travellers going to Egypt, became for a brief period the rich capital of a caravan empire. It was the trade in incense from southern Arabia and Somaliland which was their undoing, for the ambitions of the Romans to control supplies led to their occupation of Petra in AD 106 and the ultimate diversion of the caravans to other routes.

54 Petra, Jordan. El Deir

El Deir, 'the Monastery', apparently a huge two-storey temple, is cut from the end of a mountain of red-brown rock. The broken pediment and second-storey miniature *tholos*, or circular temple, recall the famous Kasneh at the entrance to Petra, but El Deir is much bigger, 140 feet high. Its single chamber is the only one in Petra to contain an altar. Public rituals were held here, for the remains of seating have been found on the flat grass sward before the temple.

El Deir is on the high northern rim of Petra, reached by way of Nabataean staircases cut in the rock of a narrow ravine. From it the eye sweeps far over the Great Rift Valley, catching what is thought to be the site of Aaron's Grave on the top of Mount Hor in the distance.

55 Petra, Jordan. Tomb façade

The tall attached columns and doorway pediment of this tomb are an elegant example of the Hellenistic or Roman influence in Petra. But the stepped battlement motifs in relief above, frequent in Petra, are decorations peculiar to the Nabataean kingdom.

56 Bosra, Syria. Columns in the Forum

Elegant Corinthian columns rise from the rubble of dressed masonry — all that remains of a once vast Forum. Vestiges of a decorated entablature suggest the fine buildings in which the secular affairs of the city were once conducted.

The caravans which left Petra for the north would call at Jerash beyond Amman and then, across the present border of Syria, at the ancient city of Bosra. At that time (from 71 BC) Bosra was the capital city of the Nabataeans, prosperous, with rich markets, palaces, temples and defensive walls. When the Romans took it in AD 105 the city was the natural capital for their new province of Arabia. Under Trajan, from AD 222 to 235, it was enlarged and given a new, grandiose title, *Nova Trajana Bostra*. It was a metropolis still under Philip (AD 245–9) and it is the ruins of the Roman past which speak today of the glory which died here thirteen centuries ago.

57 Bosra, Syria. Roman triumphal arch

An elegant triumphal arch, one of several in Bosra, stands at the end of the main street, looking out into the plain on which the city stands. The arch is decorated with niches and pilasters, one of which carries a Latin inscription.

58 Palmyra, Syria. The Temple of Bel beyond standing columns

'The greatest quantity of ruins we had ever seen,' said Robert Wood in the eighteenth century of the view which opened to him as he approached Palmyra through the Valley of the Tombs. He would be looking, as the photographer was when he took this photograph, across a waste of tumbled stone and solitary Corinthian columns towards the huge Temple of Bel, enclosed in a courtyard 200 yards square. Leading to it is the finest remaining Roman colonnaded avenue, with a triumphal arch and 150 of its 375 superb columns still standing.

Beyond the ruins, towards the Euphrates, Robert Wood saw 'a flat waste, as far as the eye could reach, without any object which showed either life or motion'. Palmyra lies out in the desert, midway between the Euphrates and the seaports of the Lebanon, and owes its origin, no doubt, to the needs of the caravan trade. It was because of its location on the edge of the Roman Empire that Palmyra briefly flourished as a kind of neutral and semi-independent buffer city between the Empire and the territory of the Parthians. At its heyday, in the third century A D, under Odenathus and his widow, the legendary Queen Zenobia, Palmyra grew rich and powerful, as a city in which the goods of two hostile powers might be exchanged. But Zenobia's ambitions alarmed Rome and led to her downfall, and that of Palmyra with her.

59 Bosra, Syria. The Roman theatre
Now restored from the Arab fortresses which were built around it, the stepped theatre at Bosra is thought to be the most completely preserved example of a Roman theatre in the world. It was huge, with a diameter of 79 yards, built to accommodate the audience of a small stadium and divided, apparently, into three sections to correspond with the three ranks of the society of the day.

60–1 Jerash, Jordan. The Roman Forum
Inside the south gate of Jerash stands the remarkable elliptical Forum, with its sweeping Ionic colonnade and the paved floor across which the westering sun here casts long shadows. In the background to the left the slender and elegant columns of the Temple of Artemis just touch the skyline; to the right the colonnaded street continues to the centre of the Roman city.

Ancient Gerasa was founded, some say, in the fourth century B C by Alexander the Great or one of his officers. It lies north of Amman on the inland caravan route from Petra to Damascus and must at one time have been under the influence of the Nabataeans. By the beginning of the Christian era it was a wealthy commercial centre and a member of the league of cities east of the Jordan. But, like Petra, it was taken over by Rome. What remains today of its former splendour stems from the Romans of the first and second centuries A D.

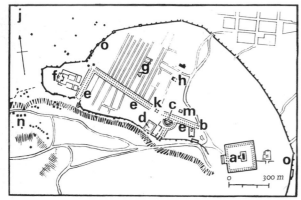

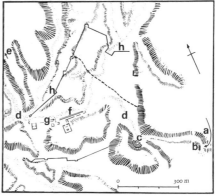

PALMYRA
a Temple of Bel (Temple of the Sun)
b Monumental Arch
c Theatre
d Agora
e Colonnade
f Diocletian's Camp
g Byzantine Basilicas
h Temple of Baalshamin
j Arab Fort
k Tetrapyle
m Baths of Diocletian
n Valley of Tombs
o Zenobia's Wall (new towers added by Justinian)

PETRA
a Entrance from Al-ji, through the Sik
b El-Kasneh, the Treasury of Pharaoh
c The Roman Theatre
d Wadi Musa
e Route to El Deir
f Street of the Town
g Site of Triple Roman Arch
h Town walls

JERASH
a Triumphal Arch of Hadrian at the approach from Amman
b Hippodrome
c South Gate
d Forum
e Temple of Jupiter
f South Theatre
g North Theatre
h Temple of Artemis
j Cathedral
k Nymphaeum
m Eastern Baths
n Western Baths
o Synagogue
p Churches
q North Gate
r River Chrysorrhoas
s Circassian village
t Town walls, enclosing 235 acres

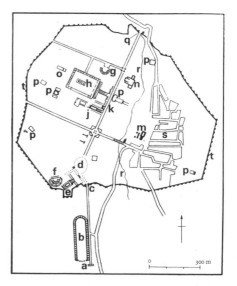

RUIN ON RUIN

In the ruin-loving dreams of western man . . . it is Greece and Italy which have always mainly enshrined those wistful, backward-gazing dreams. Perhaps because it was there that our civilization was cradled and grew; we yearn back to these vestiges of our past. Perhaps because we have been bred in a classical culture, given from our youth up to understand that there was the glory of the world; hypnotized, our eyes dazzle with it. Here were Socrates, Plato, Pericles, Praxiteles; here was Troy, here Athens, the Islands, there Magna Graecia, and the tremendousness of Rome. Nothing can compete. . . . In Ionia, the mind hankers after the resplendent past; these proud Greek cities and shrines were too good to be thrown down, to be taken by Croesus, Cyrus, Darius, ruled by Ptolemies, misruled by Seleucids, engulfed by Rome, ravaged in turn by Arabs, earthquakes, Turks, Crusaders, Mongols, Turks again; too great to lie ruining where once they stood triumphing. . . .

There is, and will be, no end to the disinterment of ruined antiquity in Asia Minor, for more, no doubt, is under the ground than above it. In Anatolia, and particularly in Pamphylia, between the Taurus mountains and the sea, cities are being extricated from the deep layers of drifted sand, grown over with shrubs and trees, that has buried them for a thousand years; Greek and Roman cities, with their temples and paved streets and shops and great theatres so deep sunk that only their top seats show. . . . Every few miles . . . the remnants of broken greatness, of theatres, walls, pillars, temples, all the splendid relics of Greece in Asia Minor, but more magnificent, in their prime, than the buildings of Hellas. Engulfed by Persia, Macedonia, Seleucia, Rome, Byzantium, Islam, they were by turns fortified, cherished, adorned, plundered, ruined, new built, annihilated. Barbarians from the east swept over them; Saracens, Turks, Armenians, Greeks, living in dying cities let them die; their marbled ruins were robbed to build mosques and mean medieval villages. The tumbled columns, the Greek and Roman inscribed entablatures, such western travellers as went that way found thrown among thickets and wildernesses, eyed with apathy and ignorance, taken for drinking-troughs, steps and seats, by a local peasantry as far below understanding or wonder as their own camels. . . .

Ruin on ruin Troy lies, and for centuries lay, among the other ruins on Troy plain, and travellers for a thousand years or so were happily confused as to what they saw, taking for Priam's Troy the glorious sea-washed columns and palaces of Alexandria Troas, founded after Alexander's death on the shore miles away. 'How was it possible', Gibbon demanded severely, 'to confound Ilium and Alexandria Troas?' But it was, until the great nineteenth-century Trojan excavations, only too possible, and to go into Trojan raptures among the broken pillars and magnificent vaulted arches standing by the sea's edge has always been among the more stirring ruin-pleasures. . . .

Layer below layer, theory after theory, have been during the last eighty years exposed; and now we see the ruins of the great Mycenaean walls and towers of Homer's Troy unearthed, standing among the later Hellenic walls, and those of the great Roman city built on these. All are marked with their successive periods; in imagination city after city rises over that wide and stony plain, looking across the Scamander to Sigeum and the sea. It is a tremendous sight. Not picturesque; not even beautiful; but magnificent in its domination, and in its evocation of the greatest legend of history. Such a pleasure, as Lady Mary Wortley Montagu observed, to see the site of what had been the greatest city of the world. But Lady Mary was too early. The Hissarlik mound was in her day yet undug, and she, shrewder and less confused than most of her contemporaries, wrote, 'All that is left of Troy is the ground on which it stood, for, I am firmly persuaded, whatever pieces of antiquity may be found round it are much more modern, and I think Strabo says the same thing.' However, she derived pleasure from seeing 'the point of land where poor old Hecuba was buried', and the burial place of Achilles, 'where Alexander ran naked round his tomb, which no doubt was a great comfort to his ghost'. . . . She enjoyed too Alexandria Troas, which she conjectured to be the remains of the city begun by Constantine for his projected capital; she 'took the pains of rising at two in the morning to view coolly these ruins which are commonly shewed to strangers . . . where 'tis vulgarly reported Troy stood.' Hiring an ass, she made a tour of the ancient walls, which were of vast extent, and was delighted with all she saw and surmised. So, indeed, must all have been who, looking on Alexandria Troas and less well informed than Lady Mary, took these romantically beautiful ruins for old Troy. On the whole our ancestors, intoxicated with this agreeable delusion, probably enjoyed themselves more than we. . . .

As to Ilium itself, it is a city of the ancestral mind; its cycle of tales rings down the centuries, the holy mythos of Hellenes and Romans, the great romantic legend of the Middle Ages, the ancestor of all the later Troys. It is not the mighty excavated walls on Hissarlik that dominate the Troad plain; it is the memory of the battling and the siege, the Trojans behind their walls, the Greeks encamped without, the slain heroes, the crafty horse, the victory and the flaming fall, the greatness and the ruin of sacked Troy. . . . Travellers, from Homer onward, have gazed on Troy and on Troy's ruins because Troy was great, but more because Troy was ancient, ruined and fallen. They would have preferred, we should prefer now, to see the great city as she was; but, gazing on her ruins, we build her in our minds.

As also we build Tyre. Since the vindictive passion of Ezekiel against Tyre some twenty-six centuries back produced one of the major Hebrew poems of invective, the reports of Tyre's death have always been exaggerated. Ruined she has been, again and again; and diminished she is; but always she has risen again, Phoenician, Roman, medieval, modern, standing on her successive ruins in the sea.

The prophet's wishful 'thou shalt be built no more' has never come to pass, though generations of visitors to Tyre have mournfully repeated the words as they gazed on the fallen fishing city; to do so is one of the Tyrian pleasures. . . . In Tyre Phoenician and Roman lie mingled . . . beautiful pillars of white and greenish marble and reddish granite lie tumbled. A great field of ruin, it slopes among thistles and coarse grass down to the sea; one may pick up stone eggs fallen from capitals, and fragments of Roman pottery and glass. Tyre has always been a magnet to travellers. Past greatness, present desolation, the legend and the ruin – the contrast is irresistible. The questionable background of ancient cursing lingers on the air. . . .

Turning from such musings, we may bathe . . . in a sandy cove, or among the fishing boats and ruins of the port and the islets beyond it, in a pearly dawn, a burning noon, or the deep violet and silver of a moon-drenched and star-glimmering night, diving among the marble foundations of the shattered piers of the crusaders' mole, among the sunk columns of Rome, among the fish and shells of drowned Phoenicia. . . .

The ruin-seeking traveller pushes on to Antioch. He is exalted, almost intoxicated, by the magnificent mountain path through the oleandrous glen of Daphne, whose gushing streams and aromatic odours and smiling ghosts from the richly licentious past, when this Cintra-like suburb was 'a perpetual festival of vice', set the right mood for the ghosts of the glory and luxury of ancient Antioch. . . . Even to this day, the visitor to Antioch and Daphne is conscious of raised spirits and a heightened sense of readiness for life's enjoyments, and this is one of the high pleasures to be derived from the ruins of Antioch. The great wall, which it is the tourist's duty and pleasure to walk round, will have, with its seven-mile circuit over crag, mountain and ravine, a bracing, tonic effect, counteracting the enervating mood of voluptuous luxury; it takes five hours of hard going. Broken and despoiled, shaken by repeated and tremendous earthquakes, plundered of its stones by Turks, Egyptians and Antiochians, nevertheless this wall of Theodosius and Justinian, raised by the crusaders to a height of fifty or sixty feet, set all its way along with strong square towers, remains one of the world's most sensational walls. It has amazed all travellers. . . . Eighteenth- and nineteenth-century travellers have found in this half-ruined grandeur a magnificence nobler than its original form. What must these walls have been, they ejaculate: but they prefer them as they are, tremendous wrecks of Golden Antioch and its splendour whose ghost marches across the ages, Seleucid, Roman, Byzantine, pagan, Christian, immortal. . . . Turning his back on seductive Antioch, one of the disciples of St Simeon Stylites set up his pillar residence some miles to the east of the city, and there sat for eight years in austere disapproval of the Antioch way of life: could he now see its desolate site, his ruin-pleasure would be great. . . .

The ruin-seeker in Anatolia . . . can travel from ruin to ruin . . . with Homer, Herodotus, Strabo, Pausanias, and several Greek poets in hand . . . he can still muse over the great Ionian cities . . . Assos and Pergamum, Cnidus and Adalia, await him; all raise the ancient question, has ruin given to such cities more than it has taken away? Their marred, piled and jumbled beauty now, their crowded bright-hued glory then, steeply towering into the same Aegean sky; the centuries have added Byzantine churches, Turkish forts; satiated with ruin, one looks back to the glorious Pergamese city of the Attalid kings, 'the throne of Satan', as the author of the Apocalypse called her (for, preoccupied by Zeus and the deified Augustus, Pergamum looked askance on the new religion). There stood the temples, the great theatre, the high altar of Zeus, the library of two hundred thousand books which Antony, that extravagant gallant, presented to his highbrow Egypt, but to whom did she bequeath them?

66 Assos, Turkey. Temple of Athena

Doric capitals from the ruined Temple of Athena lie on the shore which looks south across the Aegean Sea to the Island of Lesbos. Assos, now known as Behram, was an independent member of the Aeolian League of cities until the Persian conquest, when it was named to supply wheat to the Persian 'King of Kings'. After the death of Alexander the Great it was ruled first by Lysimachus and then by the kings of Pergamum, until finally in 130 BC it became part of the Roman Empire. Assos was one of the first Greek colonies to abandon Athena and become Christian.

67 Troy, Turkey. Fallen columns from Troy IX

Broken columns lie tumbled outside the walls of Troy, on the plain where the Greeks encamped in the legends of Homer's *Iliad*. In the corner, top right, rises the mound of Troy, all that was known of its nine cities until, in 1871, the intuitive and uninstructed excavation of Schliemann began to reveal the history which lay hidden within the tales which had rung down the centuries.

The first Troy dates from 3000 to 2500 BC. Troy II was 1000 years older than the city King Priam tried to defend. Troy III, IV and V were not really more than village settlements. Troy VI was a fine city built by new people between 1700 and 1275 BC, rich and prosperous until it was destroyed by earthquake and fire. Troy VIIA was hastily rebuilt by the survivors, with the number of people living in it enormously increased and storage space for great quantities of food and oil. Somewhere between 1240 and 1200 BC it was, in Professor Blegen's words, 'ruthlessly laid waste by the hand of man who completed his work of destruction by fire'. This was Priam's Troy.

After 500 blank years Troy VIII emerges, the Ilium of the Greeks, to be superseded by Troy IX, fully furnished with the amenities of a Roman city. It is to this last period that the fluted marble drums of the photograph probably belong, in spite of the inscription in Greek letters on the central slab.

68 Alexandria Troas, Turkey. The inner harbour

As the sun sets over the Aegean Sea, fallen columns lie on the shore of the inner harbour of Alexandria Troas. As its name implies, Alexandria was conceived, and its site at the southern corner of the plain of Troy selected, by Alexander the Great, though it was left to Antigonus to carry out the building. It was a flourishing city in Roman times and was visited twice by St Paul, who restored Eutychus to life there. Today, the ruins of a theatre, gates, arches and a Roman aqueduct can still be seen.

69 Tyre, Lebanon. Fallen columns by the shore

The ruins of Tyre lie on the Mediterranean shore of southern Lebanon, partly on the ancient fortress island and partly on the mainland to which the island is now connected. Their history goes back to the fourteenth century BC; the causeway to the island was first built by Hiram, who helped with the building of Solomon's temple. Tyre became a flourishing Phoenician fishing port and naval base, famous for Tyrian purple which it obtained from the shell-fish of its shores. Its

island fortress, freely open to the sea, made it strong, and it withstood a five years' siege by the Assyrians in the eighth century BC and a thirteen years' siege by Nebuchadnezzar in the sixth. It was finally reduced and its inhabitants massacred or sold into slavery by Alexander the Great in 332 BC. The new city, with a temple built by Herod, grew slowly, to be destroyed again by the Moslems after the fall of Acre.

70 Antioch, Turkey. The city walls

The great walls of Antioch run over the hills which look down upon the town, situated in a beautiful and fertile plain on the left bank of the Orontes. They were first built in the early centuries BC, repaired by the Byzantine emperors and raised to 50 or 60 feet high by the Crusaders. The remains of square-towered strong-points can still be seen at intervals. The city of Antioch was founded in the fourth century BC by Seleucus I Nikator, who named it for his father Antiochus, the Macedonian general. In Roman times (after 64 BC) it was the seat of the Syrian governors and an important commercial centre. Antioch is frequently mentioned in the New Testament (it was here that the followers of Jesus were first called Christians), but the town was also notorious for the profligacy of its pagan population.

71 Pergamum, Turkey. The theatre

The huge theatre of Pergamum was cut into the side of the first slopes of the Acropolis, its seventy-eight rows of seats reaching down to a vast colonnaded terrace supported on arches built into the rock. Though the theatre was built (or rebuilt) in Roman times, the Acropolis was already a striking architectural achievement before the beginning of the Christian era. It was planned and constructed by the Attalid dynasty, the active and able philosopher-kings who secured control after the death of Alexander the Great (323 BC) and raised Pergamum to a wealthy and powerful state. They reigned until 133 BC, when Attalus III, having no son, bequeathed his kingdom to Rome. The major ruins which survive are the work of the Romans, especially of the time of Hadrian and Antoninus Pius (AD 117–161).

72 Pergamum, Turkey. The library and north portico of the Asklepieion

A long colonnade runs round two sides of the main precinct of the Asklepieion, or temple-hospital, of Pergamum. Its columns, now partially re-erected, were originally an ornate Ionic, but some were replaced by examples of the Composite order after the earthquake of about AD 175. At its eastern end stood a library (from which this photograph is taken), its walls lined with recesses for the books. It was encrusted with coloured marbles and had 'windows' of thin translucent sheets of marble and alabaster.

Pergamum was one of the most important centres of the cult of Asklepios, god of healing, its influence being especially high during the second century AD, when Galen studied and practised medicine there. The cult was a combination of ritual and more practical benefits, involving much bathing (including mud-baths) and the 'temple sleep', when the patients expected the god to bring them healing dreams. Three springs supplied medicinal waters.

73 Pergamum, Turkey. Pump Room of the Asklepieion
The undercroft or crypt of the most remarkable building of the Asklepieion, the 'Pump Room', was probably the most important 'ward' of the temple. It was connected to a vaulted underground passage nearly 100 yards long, by which patients reached it from the great square and under which water ran from the main spring to the intricate water system and stone baths of the room itself. In a second storey to the building, now perished, six apses radiated from the central core and the whole was enclosed in a circular frame with two entrances.

ANTIOCH
Part of the city walls in 1799

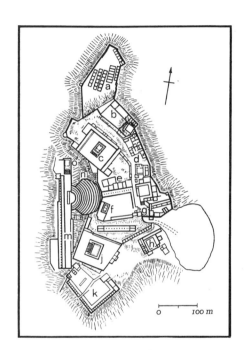

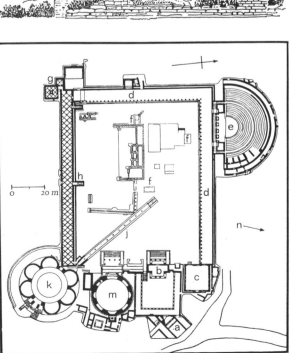

PERGAMUM *Acropolis*			
a	Store Houses	f	Temple of Athena
b	Barracks	g	Gateway
c	Temple of Trajan	h	Heroön
d	Royal Palaces	j	Altar of Zeus
e	Library	k	Agora
		m	Colonnaded Terrace
		n	Theatre
		o	Temple of Juno

PERGAMUM *Asklepieion*			
a	Sacred Way	f	Springs
b	Propylaeum	g	Latrines
c	Library	h	Subvault of Portico
d	Porticoes	j	Cryptoporticus
e	Theatre	k	Pump Room
		m	Temple of Zeus-Asklepios
		n	Direction of Acropolis (approx. 3 miles)

II Ghostly streets

THE PHANTOM TOWNS

Of all ruins, possibly the most moving are those of long-deserted cities, fallen century by century into deeper decay, their forsaken streets grown over by forest and shrubs, their decadent buildings, quarried and plundered down the years, gaping ruinous, the haunt of lizards and of owls. Such dead cities stir us with their desolate beauty, in contrast with their past greatness and wealth. . . . This plain was a plaza; there stood a temple; of the whole scarcely any traces remain; the towers which soared into the air have given way under their great weight. This broken amphitheatre is covered with the yellow jara-mago. . . . Oh fable of time, showing how great was its greatness and is now its ruin. Here came Trajan and Hadrian; the marble and gold of palaces, the laurel and jasmine of gardens, are now brambles and lagoons; the house built for Caesar is now dwelt in by lizards. . . .

Forty-five miles from Rome, in the Pontine marshes, lies Ninfa, that strange little abandoned ramparted green city round a stream, at the foot of the steep height on which the citadels of Norma and Norba are poised. Ninfa . . . is sprawled over with greenery . . . the greenery, once a wild thicket, has been, during the past century, taken in hand and turned into a very beautiful wild garden by its ducal owners, the Gaetani family. It is exuberantly, fantastically lovely and strange. An early Middle Age town (it seems to enter history in the sixth century), it played a part in the feudal, papal and imperial wars of its time, passed from hand to hand, was made a fortress in the eleventh century, was sacked by Frederick Barbarossa in the twelfth, presented to the Gaetani by a pope in the thirteenth, and steadily declined, owing to the malaria of its marshes, from the fifteenth on. Between 1670 and 1675 there were reported to be a few inhabitants still living in it, no doubt very ill. In 1681 it was seen to be deserted and invaded by trees, ivy and shrubs; the inhabitants had all fled from its miasmas to more healthy airs, carrying their possessions in ox-carts. For some years its buildings were quarried for stone, then finally abandoned to invasion of the woodland growths; the ivy, the vine, the creeping plants, covered them up; the young trees sprouted from their walls. In spite of an attempt a century later to exorcise its fevers, Ninfa remained a malarial swamp. A garden was made of the ruinous town; a new palace built, a mill set going; it was no use. Ninfa lay crumbling and deserted between its crenellated medieval walls, its ruined churches, noblemen's castles and houses, streets and dwellings and monastery walls, disintegrating beneath their mantle of green, beside the clear cold stream and little lake where once had stood a temple of the nymphs.

The stream runs, swift and strong and clear, through the jungled town; beside its banks rise square, green-wreathed towers, castle keeps, the vaulted walls and broken apses of Romanesque churches with peeling, overgrown frescoes; among them wind green lanes that were streets (their names have been recovered) and round them stand the old battlemented walls, for the most part still upright beneath their ivy coats, with their moats of running water beside them. The main street ends in an open space that was once a market place, is now a meadow. In the walls are still some gates, over the stream still two ancient bridges. One of the little palaces has been restored and is now lived in by the Duke and Duchess of Sermoneta. All the garden town is a mass of tangled sweetness and crowding shrubs and flowers.

This strange and charming place has always given intense pleasure to visitors. Among those who have surrendered themselves to its sensuous attractions are Augustus Hare and, before him, the great Gregorovius, whose enthusiastic German mind and sensibilities were wholly captured; even, it could be said, overturned. He felt the most delicious *Ruinenempfindung*, from the moment when, looking down over the Pontine marshes from the romantic heights of Norma, he caught a view of

'a great ring of ivy-mantled walls, within which lay curious mounds and hillocks, apparently made of flowers. Grey towers stood up out of them, ruins, all garlanded with green, and from the midst of this strange circle we could see a silver stream hurrying forth and traversing the Pontine marshes. . . . I asked, amazed, what that most puzzling great garland of flowers, that mysterious green ring, could be. "Nympha, Nympha," said our host. Nympha! then that is the Pompeii of the Middle Ages, buried in the marshes – that city of the dead, ghostly, silent. . . . Assuredly it has a more charming aspect than Pompeii with its staring houses, like half-decayed mummies dragged from amongst volcanic ashes and set up all around. But a fragrant sea of flowers waves above Nympha; every wall is veiled with green, over every ruined house or church the god of spring is waving his purple banner triumphantly. . . . Flowers crowd in through all the streets. They march in procession through the ruined churches, they climb up all the towers, they smile and nod to you out of every window-frame, they besiege all the doors. . . . You fling yourself down into this ocean of flowers quite intoxicated by their fragrance. The lake might have come out of the world of shadows of the Iliad or the Aeneid. The dark tower and others cast their trembling images down upon the still waters of this pool. The reeds rustled sadly. . . . You should sit here when evening bathes, first in purple then in gold, these ivied halls and ruins. I will say no word about it, nor will I try to describe it when the moon rides forth across the sky and the fairies dance in circles. . . .'

An acute case of ruin-pleasure to the head. This romantic place found its spiritual home in the romantic soul of the learned, picturesque and ivy-loving historian of the Middle Ages. Some other visitors have found it just a little too lush. But, if you like crumbling medieval ruins overgrown by wild greenery now tamed into a beautiful garden, then Ninfa is precisely what you will like. In winter and by night it has been said to be both melancholy and alarming; mist swathes the phantom town, reptiles and rodents glide about, pursued by rapacious and hooting owls, and the atmosphere is eerily bewitched. The careful and orderly guardianship of the last years may, however, have modified this effect. It may, too, have reduced the apprehension felt formerly that weather and vegetation would in time totally disintegrate the ruins, dragging them down to moulder in the damp earth until they become one with it.

The Portuguese and the Spanish strewed their now abandoned cities all about the world; they lie on coasts, in dense green jungles, in wildernesses, in river swamps. Round some, such as the ruined Antigua in Guatemala, twenty-five miles from the present capital, a new town has grown up, and the ruins have to be traced and trodden among modern streets and hotels. The pleasure of Antigua, therefore, is not what it was even fifty years back. It was then a ghostly town. Wrecked by earthquake in 1773, it was rebuilt more or less, abandoned for the new capital, Guatemala, wrecked again in 1874, and left deserted in its ruin. It had itself replaced the Conquistadores' town of 1527, which was destroyed by the volcano of Agua in 1541. Antigua, founded forthwith on its site, became the glory of colonial Spain, leading for two hundred and thirty years a brilliant and resplendent life, architecturally exquisite in its Spanish colonial magnificence, with over a hundred churches and convents, two learned universities (Bernal Diaz lived and died there), the seigneurial houses of *hidalgos*, the great arcaded palace of the Captains-General whose word and sword ruled Central America, enforcing the discipline and the religion of the Conquistadores on an alien and enslaved people from Mexico to Costa Rica. Except Lima in Peru, there was no Conquest town to stand with Antigua for might, beauty and wealth, and ecclesiastical and military power. Thomas Gage, the ex-Jesuit, described it in the seventeenth century: beautiful and wealthy, with magnificent houses and churches and many palaces, the finest cathedral in Central America, scores of monasteries, a great plaza set round with colleges, hospitals, jails; it had sixty thousand inhabitants. '*Antigua Guatemala de guerreros y de clérigos, de conquistadores españoles y de Capitanes Generales. . . .'* It is the ghost of this that one sees, as one enters Antigua from the mountains and walks the flagged streets between the ruined walls of over seventy churches and convents, between the carved façades, the coloured tiles, the coats of arms, the twisted pillars of gate-posts, of deserted eighteenth-century palaces and houses, gaily coloured, often roofless, with grass and flowers and trees sprouting from the stones. The predominant colour is a soft yellow. There are magnificent palace gateways, the great broken arcades of convents, within which markets are held and women do their washing, cloister gardens with fountains in cracked stone basins, roofless churches where birds nest on the altars and shrubs sprout from flagged chancel floors, the great double-tiered arcades of the Captain-General's palace, round which the town park now grows; the old plaza with its cracked arcades, the ruined viceroys' palace overgrown with vines, the arched and sculptured portal to what was the largest cathedral of Central America, the plazas lined with eighteenth-century palaces and broken gates, the carved pillars of the Mercéd church, richly decorated with fruit and leaves, the double row of great ruined arches of the convent of Santa Clara, the ruinous façade of the church of Belén with the mountains towering behind, the busy, shouting market within the walls of the Church of Recolección, the sweet, heavy, tropical smell of fruit, the earthy smells of manure and cattle and goats. But Antigua has become self-conscious. Anglo-Saxons, English and American, cast on it the picturesque-seeking eyes of their race, and started to buy, roof, and inhabit the ruined houses. It began with an Englishwoman and her husband, who turned their house into an antique Spanish-Indian model. The example caught on, and today Antigua is full of such houses; there is a smart hotel in the park, and consciously picturesque streets.

From the antique arcades, radio incongruously blares. And over the town brood the high mauve peaks of the twin volcanoes Agua and Fuego, which have destroyed Antigua before and will perhaps destroy it again, so that even the ruins will perish. This brooding, waiting menace gives to ruined Antigua a sinister doomed fascination; the new, growing town which one resents will pass too, and in the end, perhaps soon, will lie wrecked together with the churches and palaces of old Antigua, and with that Ciudad Vieja of the conquest which perished four hundred years ago. Meanwhile, the gaping colonnades, fallen domes, broken arches and derelict plazas of Antigua give to American tourists that nostalgic pleasure which their race finds in the ancient airs from Europe that drift darkly and strangely to their nostrils from half-remembered lands, and the Maya Indians, finding the city of their conquerors decadent about them, pad about its ruined ways and make it their home, as its hutted site was their home five hundred years ago. . . .

Portuguese Goa, the old Goa, founded in 1440 by the Hindus, to replace the ancient city of the same name, became the capital of Portuguese India when Albuquerque took it in 1510, flourished richly for one century, slipped downhill, fitfully and languidly, through the next, was abandoned, little by little, in the third, and today is the most desolate of ghosts, a forest-grown deserted city, full of churches, convents and ruinous streets of houses. It has captured the imagination of all travellers, first as the rich and beautiful Portuguese colonial capital, where churches and convents and elegant houses crowded the streets and squares, and the commerce of the Oriental empire filled the harbour with shipping and the market-places with trade. Albuquerque, having conquered and massacred the Mohammedan population, filled Goa with Hindus and Portuguese, and set to work to build and fortify a noble and Christian commercial city; Goa grew in beauty, luxury and religion like a flower, rivalling Lisbon, people said, in magnificence and grace. St Francis Xavier, who lies buried there, described it thirty years after its conquest – 'Goa is a beautiful town, peopled with Christians; it has a magnificent cathedral and many other churches, and a Franciscan convent.' There were more convents soon, and more churches, and more fine buildings; into Goa flowed all the riches of the east, gold, ivory and ebony from Mozambique, carpets from the Persian Gulf, silver, pearls, indigo, sugar, silk, pepper, spices, opium and wax; there seemed no limit set to its opulent career. The princes of the east came to visit the brilliant court of the Viceroy and went away dazzled; the saying arose, 'who has seen Goa need not see Lisbon'; the luxurious city was even compared to Rome. The triumphal entries of victorious viceroys were pagan in their splendour; from the balconied seigneurial houses, typical of the late Renaissance in Spain and Portugal, with added Oriental decoration, flowers were flung down before the horses and chariots of leaders and of distinguished guests.

From its zenith, Goa's wealth and high fortune had begun by the end of the sixteenth century to decline. It had formidable and harassing trade rivals in the Dutch; cholera and hostile Deccan neighbours occurred; the population, interbred with the natives, weakened physically and mentally in stamina; luxury and a tropical climate softened their energy; their military fortifications and defences were outgrown by the city's spread. . . . In 1759 the seat of government was moved to Panjim; the houses and public buildings of Goa were abandoned and allowed to slip into decay; the population had fallen to a few hundred.

Old Goa was presently deserted and used as a quarry for the new town. It lingered on in decay, a dwindling, dying city, full of churches and convents ringing their bells across empty streets. As early as 1710 a Jesuit wrote that it was so ruined and deserted that its ancient grandeur could only be guessed from the magnificence of the convents and churches, which were still preserved with great veneration and splendour. A century later, people spoke of the shapes of streets and squares just distinguishable among ruins covered with coconut trees; the houses were a few wretched buildings in a vast solitude. In 1835 the religious Orders were dispersed, and their convents abandoned or destroyed; the last spark of life in the city was extinct; Goa was, wrote Fonseca in 1878, a wilderness infested with snakes, in which it was hard to trace the overgrown buildings. Sir William Russell, who went there with the Prince of Wales on their tour of 1877, wrote of it with melancholy interest. . . .

So, but with more detail, have all travellers to Goa written of it for the past hundred and fifty years. Its buildings have been described, its forest-grown streets traced out and reconstructed, so that we can explore the ghost of the city, knowing where we are, identifying the green streets, the embosked churches, convents and palaces, noting how the sea road runs up from the deserted quays through the graceful curiously-shaped Viceroy's Arch, erected in 1599, still bearing the arms and statue of Vasco da Gama and surrounded by coconut palms, into the jungled phantom city of Velha Goa. Near the arch stood the immense Viceroy's Palace, described by so many early visitors as of grandiose magnificence; all that remains of it is one great portal, which was cleared from the smothering forest early this century. Beyond it we enter the strange tree-shadowed city of churches and convents and roofless houses with window-panes of sliced oyster-shell. There is the great Inquisition Palace, once the largest building in Goa, with its cells and winding corridors: it was, wrote Jean Baptiste Tavernier in 1676, one of the most beautiful buildings in all the Indies; in 1827 the abbé Cottineau spoke of its *'façade de toute beauté'*, but said that the palace had been falling into ruin since, at the demand of England during the Peninsular War, the Inquisition had been abolished in the Portuguese dominions; it is now a pile of jumbled stones; there is less of it left than of the great hospital, beautiful still in its vine-grown, palm-thronged dilapidation. But the glory of Goa was and is in its churches and convents; a group of these stands in the largest square, whose outlines can be traced in the dense greenery. There is St Cajetan, modelled on St Peter's; bats hang from its chancel roof. St Augustine's towered façade is of great beauty and dignity; the body of the church is destroyed; the gaping windows and doors are swathed with vine and ivy. All these broken masks, these gaping façades, where trees thrust through windows and shrubs creep round doors and the hot sky burns beyond, give an extraordinary effect of a city enspelled, magicked, sunk in a green ocean. Around the crowd of churches and convents lie coconut groves that were city squares, wind green alleys that were streets, criss-crossing among the jungle, running, faintly traceable, beside roofless houses. The sweet scent of frangipani drifts on the warm air. A few Goanese priests come in by day to say masses in one of the mouldering churches; they do not spend the night in the ghostly, malarial city, but return to New Goa at sunset.

Old Goa induces in those who wander in it a strange form of enchanted and dream-like trance. *'Dilettevole molta e poco sana'*: so said an Italian traveller of the seventeenth century. Its historian, the enthusiastic and erudite Sr Da Silva Correia, maintains that its solitudes are heavy with the ideas and feelings of those who dwelt there once, and that these move us more greatly than the ruins themselves. *'Il est toutefois vrai'*, he wisely adds, *'que chaque voyageur éprouve des sentiments personnels en face des ruines. . . . Mais le seul mot, ruine, est capable d'éveiller des idées étranges et mystiques dans la pensée surexcitée des touristes érudits.'*

Exploring the green streets where once merchants thronged with the rich wares of the Indies, where luxurious and lazy *hidalgos* rode abroad in ornate palanquins, where their slaves were bought and sold in the market squares, where heretics walked in dire procession to that other square with its piled faggots, where, among the tangle of coconut palm, liana and vine, the ancient bells still ring out for mass, where, at every step, lies the broken, crumbling baroque beauty of old colonial Portugal, the erudite and over-excited tourist is indeed moved to the most delicious melancholy. He may feel, with Sr Correia, that old Goa should be taken in hand by archaeologists, its decay arrested before it entirely crumbles away, that buildings should be restored and roads defined before all traces are forest-drowned, that it should become a celebrated goal for travellers. Or he may feel that this would be, as nearly always, to rub the bloom from a fruit in exquisite decay, and that Velha Goa thus taken in hand would lose the peculiar rotten-ripe flavour that now enspells its phantom streets. A day will come, fears its patriotic Portuguese champion, when, if it is left abandoned and uncared-for, its ruins will be swallowed up in the earth, entirely lost in the vegetable ocean which is choking them. He is, of course, right: such a day will come, and Old Goa, the glory of colonial Portugal, will be only a memory and a forest of mounds. On the other hand, it may become a museum piece, tidy, labelled and bare, the encroaching jungle thrown back, the grass plucked from the streets and squares, the trees cut down from the church windows, the slumbering bats sent flying. Whichever of these destinies awaits it, it may be said that it is having today its finest hour. Would that it might be for ever thus preserved, caught and held in the amber moment.

Another of Albuquerque's conquests, another city which, but for how disconcertingly brief a period, enjoyed the lovely Portuguese luxury, the gorgeous Portuguese rewards of eastern commerce, as well as those, still richer, of Persia trading from her gulf – another such rich lost city, but now more lost, more sunk into the engulfing earth, was Ormuz, the ancient Hormuz, once standing on the mainland of the Persian Gulf, transferred medievally, because of Tartar raids, to the island five miles off shore where now its remains lie. The remains of the ancient mainland Hormuz, too, have been traced in the last century; extensive ruins, said Colonel Pelly, the British Resident at Bushire, who identified them, several miles up a creek, largely obliterated by cultivation; he collected from them a few ancient bricks. The sea has receded from that one-time great commercial port, the emporium of Arabia, Egypt and the Indies, whose long wharf is still faintly to be seen. Ormuz, a well-known gulf trading city from the second century A D, had later its own dynasty of small kings, its palaces and mosques and harbour. About 1300 the new island city was built; well fortified and full of costly merchandise, but hot, and the island was waterless. Ibn Batuta described it, a fine city, a great mart, on an island made of rock salt, rich with great pearls from its fisheries, spoken of through the next centuries as the world's emporium, as if it were a modern Tyre. The greedy eyes of Portugal fell on it; Albuquerque with his Portuguese squadron swooped on it, and the Persian king yielded, becoming a tributary to Albuquerque's master. The Portuguese commander built a strong fortified castle, bastioned and ramparted, on the island; it still stands there, ruined but spectacular. . . . But in 1622, after over a century of subjection, the puppet Persian ruler revolted, called in the East India Company to help him (trade rivals of Portugal, and resenting the Inquisition's burning of English merchants and seamen at Ormuz, they were also heavily bribed by 'the Duke of Shiraz'), and, after a ten weeks' siege, the Portugals surrendered castle, city and island to Persia.

Plundered and spoiled, from then on, Hormuz dwindled and decayed. . . . It was to its past glories that Milton looked back when he wrote of

> *the wealth of Ormus and of Ind,*
> *Or where the gorgeous East, with richest hand*
> *Showers on her kings barbaric pearl and gold.*

Not many years after the Persian reconquest Sir Thomas Herbert wrote a melancholy obituary. 'At the end of the isle appear yet the ruins of that late glorious city, built by the Portugals' (Herbert corrected this in a later edition), 'but under command of a titular king, a Moor. It was once as big as Exeter, the buildings fair and spacious, with some monasteries and a large bazaar or market. Of most note and excellence is the castle, well-seated, entrenched and fortified. In a word, this poor place, now not worth the owning, was but ten years ago the only stately city in the Orient. . . . The poor city is now disrobed of all her bravery; the Persians each month convey her ribs of wood and stone to aggrandize Gombroon, not three leagues distant, out of whose ruins she begins to triumph.'

A wretched hot salt island, but the Portuguese city had had many churches and friaries, stately houses, a fine bazaar, and as gallant a castle as any other in the Orient. But a ruin Ormuz became and remains. Even the bastioned castle, so much admired for so long, is now falling into decay, ravaged by the sea, its deep moat silted up. Of the city, nothing stands but a minaret; of the other buildings, all the stately houses, palaces, churches and monasteries mentioned by sixteenth- and seventeenth-century writers, only foundations remain. There is a small sea-faring and pearl-fishing population living in huts on the eastern shore; otherwise Ormuz has sunk into fantastic desolation, a ghost city haunting the strange island of red ochre ridges and low purple hills, above which tower a few high sharp peaks of gleaming white salt, as in a Doré picture. The Portugals who lived and traded and built and fortified and grew rich there cannot have enjoyed it, though in its strange tawny desolation and burning heat Castilians might feel at home. . . .

Macao was always, even in its heyday, on the road to destruction, always on its way out: 'formerly very nice and populous', said Lord Anson's chaplain in 1743, 'but at present it is much fallen from its ancient splendour'. William Hickey went on shore from his ship to see it, but found it a miserable place; Lord Macartney in 1794 commented on the neglected state of many large and costly buildings, and on the luxury which had enervated the Portuguese, giving the envious explanation of the decline and fall of foreigners. In 1857 Macao pleased Laurence Oliphant by its 'air of respectable antiquity', which was refreshing after the parvenu Hongkong. 'The narrow streets and grass-grown plazas, the handsome façade of the fine old cathedral crumbling to decay . . . the shady walks and cool grottos, once the haunt of the Portuguese poet . . . all combine to produce a soothing and tranquillizing effect.'

A little more, and Macao would slip into being a decayed city; drowsy obsolescence haunts its cobbled streets and verandahed, brightly painted houses, over which the great cathedral façade towers like a warning ghost, or like a particularly successful sham ruin closing a vista in a gentleman's landscape garden. It seems, indeed, a little curious that no English gentleman has ever, we believe, used it for a model: baroque Follies have been less used than one would expect; considering the admirable effect that a baroque, preferably churrigueresque, temple, arch or façade would produce in parks, it seems an opportunity neglected and an adornment over-due. . . .

Vanished, ruined, or decaying cities lie all over India, in their varied stages of decadence or all-but disappearance. Some, once great and prosperous, have dwindled into villages, with the shells of palaces tumbling on noble flights of steps above some lovely lake where pilgrims bathe or women come from mud hovels to wash their clothes; some, sunk in river mud, moulder on the banks of the great rivers, and crocodiles wallow in the deserted ports. Magnificent houses, stately mosques, falling yearly into deeper ruin, stand among palm-roofed huts; the mouldering palace halls shelter hovels, the jungle creeps about the streets, and the bazaars are carpeted in green. . . .

The question arises, why have so many beautiful Indian cities, ruined by enemies or abandoned by caprice, been left in their ruins through the centuries? Money has not lacked: the rich Rajahs who ruled the provinces spent lavishly on their new cities, their palaces, their courts, their queens, their pleasures, their caparisoned elephants, their armies. The traditional jewels the size of eggs, gold and silver and ivory, were tossed about like annas and rupees; Amber, Chitor, Halebid, Vijayanagar, Gaur, Mandu, a score of other exquisite ruined towns full of costly palaces and noble temples, could have been restored and inhabited, had their rulers or their conquerors been so minded. Instead, they were left to decay in beauty, the wild trees and long grass taking possession year by year, decade after decade, century after century, while only the jungle creatures and pigeons and peacocks walked the marble floors of the palaces and spread their tails on the roofs. Was it inertia, or distaste for the shattered and discarded, or for the towns of the conquered foe, or was it something subtler, the half-conscious, eternal love of ruin, *plus beau que la beauté*? Indians cannot tell you; perhaps they do not know. . . .

The people of India, Pakistan, Cambodia, Burma, Ceylon, China, carry their past cultures like heirlooms, with serene dignity. All those worlds of rich, sinister, decayed beauty encircle them like nimbuses as they go about their employs, eyes turned a little obliquely, as if they communed with a past just round the corner. Much of it is a bloody past enough; its ruins decorate the deserts and lakes and mountains of Rajputana, that battleground of ancient Hindu civilization with the waves of Moslem invaders. There wrecked Chitor, the ancient capital of the kings of Mewar in their glory, stands high on its hill, holding within its fortified broken wall the abandoned ruins of palaces, temples, streets and towers. The invaders sacked it from the fourteenth century on; Akbar took it in 1570, sacking and massacring and destroying, leaving it in ruin unrepaired, looking on the ruins with high victorious pleasure, taking away all its royal symbols, removing its gates for his capital at Akbarabad; henceforth the Mewar capital was Udaipur. Chitor lay desolate, a jumble of magnificent wreckage. Its tremendous tree-riven walls tower like a great ship above the new little town at its foot. A steep road winds up to the walls and town gates; entering in, one is in a stupendous murdered city. All about the rocky hill climb the empty palaces and temples. How fine and prosperous Chitor once looked is described in the ninth-century Khoman Rasa: 'Its towers of defence are planted on the rock, nor can their inmates even in sleep know alarm. . . . It is in the grasp of no foe. . . .'

But the foe Akbar grasped it and Jahangir installed there a traitor son of Chitor who had gone over to the Mogul foe, 'to reign among the ruins'. He did so for seven years, protected by a Mogul guard, while the wrecked city of his ancestors shamed his treachery, until at last he threw up his post and handed it over to a Rajput patriot.

If the Chitor ruins hurt this quisling, their beauty pleased the English embassy which Elizabeth sent out to Jahangir. . . .

Similar aesthetic pleasure was experienced by Colonel James Tod, learned annalist of the Rajput states, when he visited Chitor in 1822. His heart beat high as he approached the ancient capital with its reminiscences of glory, its shattered splendour. He climbed the jungled slopes which led steeply up to the rocky summit, passing through broken gates to the plateau strewn with tumbled fragments of palaces once lovely. . . .

Columns strewn, and statues fallen and cleft,
Heaped like a host in battle overthrown.

Above the city stand the richly carved Jain Towers of Victory and of Fame, intricately stairwayed, little ruined; one of them is crowned, insultingly, with a Moslem dome; from the top of either, one may look down on the vanquished, silent city asleep within its broken walls, and the blue plain stretching beyond it. Kipling gives the best description of Chitor, in *The Naulahka* and in *Letters of Marque*; the Chitor of sixty years ago. His American, Tarvin, entered it through the torn wall before the dawn . . . then came down to the streets, disturbing the squirrels and monkeys that lived in the cool dark of the empty houses, and then, it will be remembered, descended a slippery rock path into a tangle of trees that concealed a tank of stagnant green, a sinisterly chuckling drip of water, a sacred crocodile, and a terrifying cave. It is more desirable than this to walk about the palaces, with sunlight streaming through walls and roof, and climb 'crazy stone stairways, held together, it seemed, by the marauding trees', stepping delicately among the fallen sculptures and the ghosts of the Rajput men and women who died in vain and could not save their city. . . .

Many abandoned cities, such as Gaur and Pandua in Bengal, Mandu and Chandravati in Central India, and probably hundreds more, have gone down into the jungle, some to be recovered in our present age of tenderness to ancient ruins, others to be lost for ever. Gaur, one of the most magnificent in India (which is to say in the world), was, both before and after its Mohammedan conquest in 1198, the capital of Bengal, a celebrated city of beautiful buildings and high learning, splendidly walled, ten miles long, with great stone embankments. Its huge brick citadel, set with four corner towers and gate, now encloses desolation. The Golden Mosque, with arcaded corridor and brick domes, has been long since wrecked by trees growing up between its bricks, tearing it to pieces; other smaller but delightful mosques are also partly shattered; their courts grown with trees.

The tall minaret, from which the muezzin called, stands erect, shrub-grown, broken-domed; the immense walls of the palace look, in the nineteenth-century pictures, like vertical forests, a-sprout with trees; they would make easy climbing. The Dakhil Gate, in the same pictures, also supports a grove of trees on its square lintel. Broken marbles and fragments lie everywhere. For centuries deserted Gaur was plundered of its stones; scarcely a village, city or building in all the Malda district but was largely built of Gaur's ruins; Pandua, twenty miles away, which succeeded it for a time as capital is full of its sculptured stones with Hindu carvings, turned face inward and built incongruously into mosques. For their restless rulers alternated between the two capitals; always, as usual, they sought a city. Finally in 1575 Akbar's governor, struck with Gaur's charm, moved back into it with his court and people; too many people, for the density of the inhabitants caused plague to break out; flinging the corpses into the moat and lake only made things worse, and everyone who was left moved on, and that was the end of Gaur as a going concern. Pandua too, for the plague raged all around.

Both cities, and all the district, were abandoned, and jungle enveloped them. Tigers roamed the grassy streets of Gaur, and lurked in the forests that edged the road to Pandua; approach was dangerous. All about lay a wild country, uneven with buried ruins. Across a forest path stands a lonely carved lintel, like a stile; ornamental bricks and marbles lie scattered in deep dangerous grass among the snakes.

This is how dead Gaur stood for three centuries and more. The jungle is now largely cleared and ploughed; and tigers no more pad about the tree-grown streets or leap from silent mosques. The preservation of ancient cities, so foreign a western notion, is at work; Gaur's antiquities can now be better seen, but are less becomingly clothed.

This is so in very many of the deserted cities.

Mandu, that great walled town stretching for eight miles along the high ridge of the Vindhya hills, full of glorious memorials of Pathan architecture, has suffered much the same process – Hindu and early Moslem magnificence, noble buildings, fame in the east and the west, conquests, destruction, desertion, vegetation, twentieth-century care and protection. One may have one's own preference for any among its stages; one may look back nostalgically to the days before the Moguls took over and destroyed much of the city, rebuilding it with Hindu materials; or to the glorious Moslem centuries of fame, learning, conquest and wealth . . . or one may wistfully hanker after the three centuries of picturesque and dendrofied ruin; or one may opt for twentieth-century clarity. The dendrofied ruin is not to be preferred by the clear and intelligent mind; yet it stirs the imagination as no tidied-up and labelled antiquities can. When we read, about the ruined, the long lost, the almost vanished city of Chandravati near Ahmedabad, 'Nature herself, so prolific in these regions, is rapidly covering the glories of the Pramaras with an impenetrable veil. The silence of desolation reigns among these magnificent shrines, and the once populous streets, which religion and commerce united to fill with wealthy votaries, are now occupied by the tiger and the bear, or the scarcely more civilized Bhil' – the heart leaps up to hail tiger and bear and Bhil and prolific nature; one is delighted to read further that 'the city itself is now overgrown with jungle; its fountains and wells choked up, its temples destroyed, and the remains daily dilapidated by the Girwur chief who sells the marble materials to any who have taste and money to buy them.' That was in 1824. The gifted discoverer and explorer, Colonel Tod . . . enjoyed similar pleasures all about India, resurrecting lost cities out of old chronicles, from the contemporary reports of Arabian travellers, and from local tradition. He discovered Anulwarra, by the Gulf of Cambay, that ancient Jain capital founded in 740 and growing at once into magnificence, great in trade, schools, learning, temples, palaces, and a 'sea of men'; in the eleventh and twelfth centuries it dominated eighteen countries. Every Jain and Brahmin temple was destroyed by convert Moslem rulers. . . . 'The sanguinary Alla', who had razed walls, temples and palaces, had even ploughed up the ground. Anulwarra lingered on, its power and prosperity dead. 'With its discovery', Colonel Tod exulted, 'years of anxiety terminated' (for his life was passed in these anxious quests, these happy finds); 'here is the site of the first city of Vansraj.'

All Colonel Tod's deserted cities were, however densely jungled, above the ground.

There are, all over north India, more ancient cities still, buried layer below layer, town below town, to be dug up almost by chance by archaeologists in search of early civilizations. The great Indus valley is the centre of such a pre-Aryan civilization, perhaps flourishing there five thousand years ago, building cities and temples of brick, laying out streets, nearly four thousand years before the Aryans flooded in. Excavation during the last thirty years has exposed one of these cities – or rather a pile of such cities, each climbing on the wreckage of the city below it. Mohenjo-Daro, the Indians call it, 'the city of the dead'; it lies in the dreary wastes of Sind, on the borders of Baluchistan. It is an impressive sight: great grass-grown streets thirty feet wide and three-quarters of a mile long, bordered with huge blocks of brick that were walls and houses, stupas and an enormous bath. This top city perhaps dates from 2,750 BC; older foundations lie below it. From these jewellery, pottery, gold and silver, and terra-cotta toys have been reclaimed, and coins from far lands. It seems that trade flourished; as for the town drainage and water system, it appears to have been as efficient as that of Knossos. It became a Buddhist city, as the stupas show. The Indians of the Indus make pilgrimages to the ruins seeking treasure; there are still acres of mounds not fully excavated, and no one knows what will be revealed on the deepest levels.

Mohenjo-Daro is no object of beauty; its antiquarian interest is immense. . . .

The Mogul invaders from the north ruined great Vijayanagar, the magnificent capital of a great kingdom, the glory of south India; its magnificence, wealth and state were the talk of Asia and Europe, its buildings, secular and profane, of fabulous splendour and grace, the kings and their thousands of elephants and wives. The city, stretching south from the river Tungabhadra, covered many square miles, a resplendent glitter of palatial glory, temple towers, baths, fountains, pavilions, gardens and lakes, and streets thronged with elephants and men. Sacked and battered by the Moslem armies in 1565, Vijayanagar fell; fleeing inhabitants escaped with much gold and jewellery, many elephants, and as much of their portable property as possible; most of the citizens and most of the wealth went down with their city before the ravening Mogul army. The great area of the populous capital became a desolate space, strewn with the ruins of buildings once splendid, now mostly past identification, fragments of Dravidian architecture in rich profusion. Hampi, the old original core of Vijayanagar on the river, is still lived in and is full of temples, and a place of pilgrimage. But no one, in the four centuries of its ruin, has tried to rebuild Vijayanagar, nor, it seems, will.

Gaur, India. Detail of the carved door of the Firoz Minar, 1488

84 Antigua, Guatemala. Capital in the Cathedral
A sculptured angel and intricate scroll-work still rise above the decorated capital of a pier in the nave of the cathedral. The arches no longer support the dome, which fell, together with the central part of the nave, in the earthquake of 1773. Ciudad Vieja, the 'Old City' of the Conquistadores, was destroyed in 1541 by the volcano Agua which towers high above it. In its place rose Antigua, for 230 years a brilliant centre of colonial Spain with 60,000 inhabitants. On 29 July 1773 the city was shattered by a tremendous earthquake; attempts to rebuild it were wrecked again in 1874 and its ruins were deserted. A new capital, Guatemala City, rose twenty-five miles away.

85 Antigua, Guatemala. Façade of Nuestra Señora de los Remedios
A ruined façade stands in the hot sunlight, its superimposed columns and the broken images in the niches of its wall still displaying the rich Baroque of the Spanish colonial style.

86 Goa, India. Arch of the Immaculate Conception
An arched entry stands, squat and massive, among the coconut palms that have engulfed Old Goa. Its four fluted Corinthian pillars, heavy entablature and stone cross are intact, witnesses to the dignity and wealth of the Portuguese colonial capital of the sixteenth century. Goa, an ancient site, was taken from its Mohammedan masters in 1510, by the famous Portuguese admiral Affonso d'Albuquerque. Within a few years it was an opulent city compared even with Rome. But it was not to last; in two more centuries the city, ravaged by cholera, was ruined and deserted, its trade gone.

87 Goa, India. The Basilica of Bom Jesus
A high stone cross stands before the Goan Jesuit church which houses in its sacristy the body of St Francis Xavier. It was built at the expense of Dom Jeronymo de Mascarenhas, a Captain of Cochin and Ormuz who is buried within, and consecrated in 1605. Each holy day, in this deserted city in the jungle, at least until the Indian invasion, priests came from the new Goa to say mass, their rich ornaments and golden robes defended by a Portuguese sentry at the door, his bayonet fixed.

88 Hampi, India. Monkey goddess
Carved in bold relief, as tall as a man, the monkey goddess and royal symbol of the Vijayanagar kings stands near the entrance to Hampi's nine square miles of ruins. It is the mark of the dynasty which, established in 1336, stopped the Moslem invaders for over two hundred years. Their capital, Vijayanagar, 'City of Victory', was described by contemporary writers as the finest and most populous city of sixteenth-century India. It was taken finally by the Moslem armies in 1565, sacked and left to decay.

89 Macao, China Coast. Cathedral of St Paul
The empty façade of Macao's cathedral is still the most imposing reminder of the time when Portugal planted this outpost on the China Coast and the rich spice trade of the East made it flourish. It was built (by Japanese Christian workmen) in 1638, in a rich Portuguese Baroque style with dynamic clusters of superimposed columns, and remained the cathedral of the province until the 1830s when it was destroyed by fire, leaving only the west front.

90 Gaur, India. The Camkatti Mosque
Brick-built, except for its stone base, its narrow door topped by a pointed arch, this mosque is typical of the architectural style which developed in Moslem Bengal of the fifteenth century. Stone was difficult to obtain and Hindu influence was strong, for Gaur was a famous capital of the Hindus long before the Mohammedan conquest in 1198. It grew to a city stretching for nearly twenty miles along what was once the high bank of the Ganges, its suburb, and alternate capital, Pandua, forming the northern end.

91 Pandua, India. Wall decoration on the Adina Mosque
Elaborate floral panels and patterned string-courses in moulded brick relieve the exterior façade of the great Adina Mosque at Pandua. The mosque is 507 feet long and 285 feet wide; inside, eighty-nine arched openings led onto a centre courtyard. The roof of the cloisters has now fallen; it was supported by the walls and some 260 massive pillars and consisted of no less than 378 identically designed domes. Attached to the outer wall towards the north-west corner stand the ruins of the tomb of the illustrious Abdul Mujahid Sikander Shah, King of Persia and Arabia, who built the mosque and dedicated it on 14 February 1369.

92 Hampi, India. By the Tungabhadra river
Though the country of the Vijayanagar kings was rich, their capital was on barren ground. Huge boulders lay in heaps or stuck singly out of the ground. The river Tungabhadra runs along the north of the ruins; at this point, one of the sacred stretches, it takes a great sweep north. In the middle distance a wide road runs past flat-roofed pavilions, to end in a stepped incline up to a temple in the rocks.

93 Hampi, India. Pavilion and rice fields
Through the smoke of burning stubble, an open pillared pavilion reaches to the skyline. The columns which stand on the low platform are in the highly ornate style of Vijayanagar.

94 Ninfa, Italy. The town beyond the lake
Across the silent lake of Ninfa rises the grey, battlemented tower of the thirteenth-century castle, built by Pietro di Roffredo Gaetani. Around it, hidden by the tangled trees and flowers, lie the ruins of the ducal town. In the eleventh century Ninfa, in the Pontine Marshes near Rome, was a feudal fortress, engaging in war. It suffered assault and capture by Frederick Barbarossa in the twelfth, revived as the flourishing seat of the Gaetani family and then slowly died, the victim of an unseen and persistent enemy, the malaria from its stagnant waters.

95 Hampi, India. The Virupaksha temple reflected in a pool
The gopuram or tall entrance tower of the temple which holds the idol of Virupaksha is reflected in a pool of the

Tungabhadra water which runs through the centre of the shrine. The tower is 120 feet high, built of stepped tiers of multiple pillars, in which the central shaft is surrounded by a group of slender columns all emerging from the same decorated base. The whole is surmounted by a highly decorated horseshoe-shaped dome.

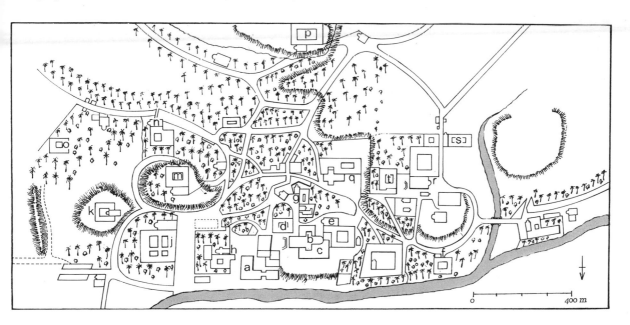

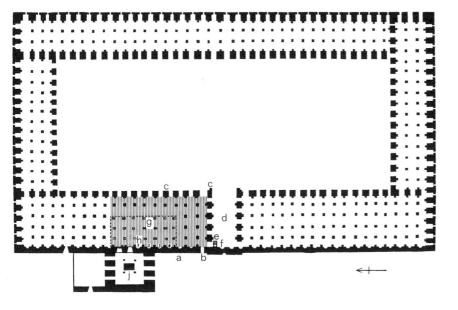

PANDUA

The Adina Mosque

a	Outer wall
b	Entrance
c	Arches of inner court
d	Transept
e	Pulpit in transept
f	Prayer niche in transept
g	King's Throne or Royal Gallery
h	Prayer niches on Royal Gallery
j	Ruins of Tomb of Sikander Shah

GOA

a	Viceroy's Palace
b	Cathedral
c	Archiepiscopal Palace
d	Inquisition Palace in Ruins
e	Convent and Church of St Francis
f	College of St Bonaventure
g	Houses and Churches of Misericordia
h	Convent and Church of St Cajetan
j	Convent and Church of St Dominic
k	Church and House of Nossa Senhora de Monte
m	Convent and Church of the Carmelites
n	College and Church of St Paul
o	Hospital of St Lazarus
p	Convent and Church of the Miraculous Cross
q	House and Church of Bom Jesus
r	Convent and Church of St Augustine
s	College of the Augustinians
t	Convent and Church of St John of God

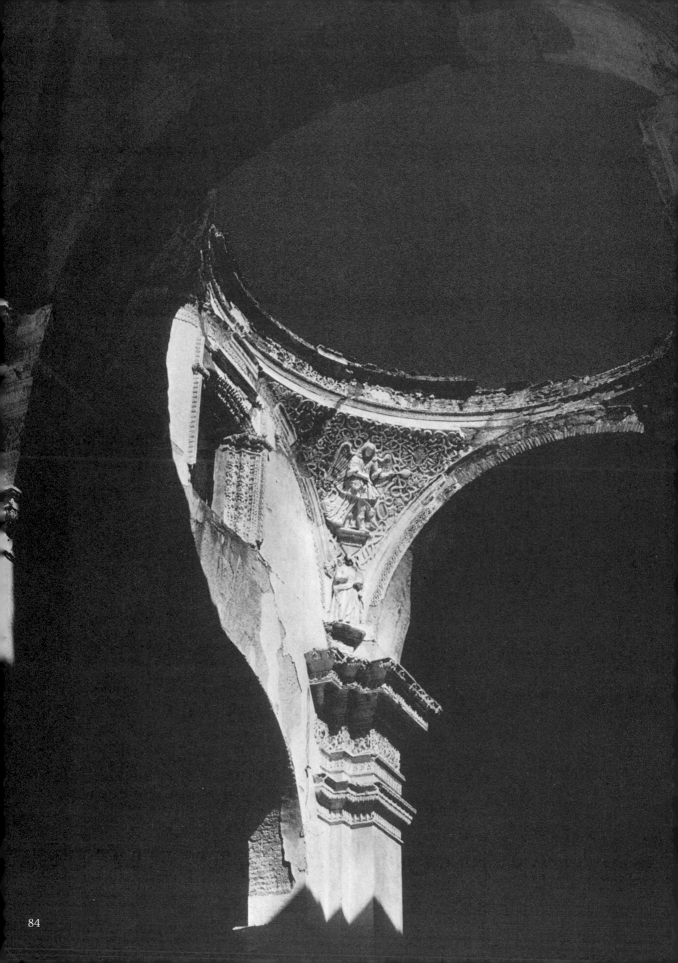

CITIES ENSPELLED

All about Central and South America the green dusk embosks the lost cities of Americans, not the Americans our late colonists, our present benefactors and defenders, but the Americans before them, who built in the deep heart of great forests, built carved stone cities, palaces, temples, tombs, abandoned them and moved on to build fresh cities somewhere else, leaving cities, temples, palaces, tombs, to sink into the jungle, to become part of that encroaching green, often to be no more found or seen, sometimes to be discovered by travellers of other races many centuries later. . . . But, whether Toltec, Aztec, Yucatan, Mayan, or whatever, whether dating from the seventh century or the fifteenth, whether deserted at the coming of the Spanish, or long before, or even after, whether dedicated to the cult of the Quetzalcoatl or any other gods, whether belonging to the 'best period' or the less good, whether sunk and obliterated in dense jungle, or standing in clearings, whether on mountains or on plains or set round great lakes or on some almost unvisited sea coast (such as those found by turtle fishers buried in the drifting sands of a sickle-shaped bay on the Vera Cruz coast, and visited in 1927 by Dr Thomas Gann), whether magnificent like Chichen Itza, Palenque, Copan, Uxmal, Tula, Teotihuacan, Tikal, Menche, and others, or small palaces and temples of a poor period dug out of the jungle in fragments, all these American Indian medieval cities, so engulfed, so dendrofied, so mysterious, so massive and so ornate, so haunted by the ghosts of gods and men who still dwell there, so intent on hastening back into the reaching arms of the forest that stretch to hold them, have an attraction that is partly fear. They are beautiful in themselves; they must have been beautiful unruined, as described by the Spaniards who first saw them – 'All the temples and palaces were perfectly built, whitewashed and polished outside, so that it gave pleasure to see them from a distance. All the streets and squares were beautifully paved . . .', and were still more beautiful when discovered again by travellers, with the forest growing on palace roofs and drifting into temple windows, with the rich carvings green with lichen and moss, with the ruins of Spanish houses tumbling about the monuments of the conquered races. Now that so many are cleared of forest and excavated from earth and dug out of mounds, they are still beautiful and delightful, and still haunted. To the temples, Indians still come to pray to their ancient gods.

There must be hundreds of such cities still undiscovered, still unearthed, biding their time in the depths of the primeval, perhaps now quite impenetrable, forests; cities that may never, short of some earth-shaking catastrophe of natural or human destruction, be seen again by man. Meanwhile, the descendants, the disinherited heirs, of those who built these cities, build no more. Reduced and plundered, driven from their proud towns, palaces and temples by ferocious and possessive white men, they have abandoned dwellings of stone and for centuries have taken to the woods, living in wooden cabins, sometimes putting up these in the shadow of their ancestral ruins, sometimes in forest clearings, cultivating small patches of soil. They have become barbarous; persecution, slavery and fear stunned them into apathetic lack of initiative. How could these races have built those cities, we ask. In the same way, looking at the ignorant and destructive Arabs of the deserts, we ask, was it the ancestors of this race who once dazzled and led the world of thought in science, art, letters and geography? Where, for that matter, are the heirs of the fifth-century Hellenes, or of the Romans whose empire was the known world? Such questions are idle; races go up and go down; their ruined civilizations strew the earth. . . .

The Maya forest cities and temples have not lacked their inspired reporters and artists, and to peruse the nineteenth-century volumes of ruin-seeking in Central America is like reading a series of illustrated epic poems. Excitement ran high, as well it might. For, hidden in these wild green wildernesses, lay glorious Indian cities and temples and palaces built of massive sculptured stones, once densely peopled, once the shrines of religious devotion and pilgrimage, then abandoned, who knows when, to ruin and decay, while the forest drifted over them and trees grew from windows and roofs and vines bound them about, and jackals laired in their temples, and the bright birds of the jungle whistled and hooted in their mossy halls. Either the inhabitants moved on, in the ancient Indian manner, driven by their gods or their fears, to make new settlements elsewhere, or, in many cases, they fled from their cities to escape the cruel invading Spaniards who pressed in from the coast with slaughter and slavery, and the white man's power of making life intolerable to the indigenous races whose homes he seized. 'Apparently abandoned soon after the conquest' – again and again this is the presumption about the deserted cities discovered, after three or four centuries of abandonment, by explorers. When they were built is usually a matter of dispute among archaeologists; some say early, some say late; the dating of the inscriptions has still a long way to go. Explorers have come on these forest ruins after tremendous battling with the intimidating jungle, perhaps inspired by the accounts of other explorers, perhaps almost by chance, perhaps by the identification of sites with the descriptions given by post-conquest Spaniards who had seen the cities in their full glory, or in their early ruin, as Copan in Honduras was seen and described by a Spanish officer in a letter to King Philip in 1576.

The fashion of exploring to Copan was started by John Lloyd Stephens of New Jersey, who, in 1839, having seen various references to it, set off with the artist Frederick Catherwood to struggle through the most painful tropical jungles and swamps in search of the fabulous ruins. Having fought through the green, stifling, thorn-set, poisonous and mosquito-infested hell, they at last came on the extraordinary stones – richly carved steles and pyramids, as fine in workmanship, thought Stephens, as anything in Egypt, idols, great solid walls thickly overgrown with green, temples, altars and shrines, terraces and flights of stairs, strange monuments scattered over a wide tract of forest, half buried in throttling trees; a city long lost, built when, abandoned when? Except that it was Mayan, Stephens did not know. None of the local Indians took any interest in it; one of them informed him that that part of the jungle was his land (though neither he nor anyone else had seen the ruins), and showed signs of being obstructive; Stephens bought the ruins from him for fifty dollars, celebrated his purchase with a gala party for the village, and proceeded to explore it. Later they went on into Guatemala, Chiapas and Yucatan, finding Mayan buildings scattered all about the jungles. In 1842 Stephens published his sensational account of his discoveries, illustrated by Catherwood's drawings, and Mayan ruins broke dramatically into the world's imagination. Stephens was not the first white man to visit and describe them; indeed it seems that there is seldom a first discovery of anything. Henri Mouhot's finding of Angkor was preceded by another Frenchman; Stephens' Mayan journey had been anticipated by de Waldeck's a few years earlier, and by other travellers and writers during the past three centuries; Columbus was anticipated by Norsemen; the Spanish Conquistadores by less sensational and showy colonists; the excavators of all buried cities by wandering tourists and their random spades; we too easily use the word 'discovery' when a little earth, a little vegetation, a drift of sand, has temporarily obscured buildings from view and someone takes a spade and uncovers them.

But, if there are few (and untraceable) pioneers, there are followers; after Copan and the other Central American cities and temples entered the news, explorers were drawn to the scene, excited by this extraordinary and beautiful unknown architecture. A. P. Maudslay was one of the most able and determined of these; he did not have the great pleasure, as Stephens had, of acquiring ruins by purchase, but he enjoyed himself at intervals for years, settling down by Copan with his wife and Indian workmen, pitching a tent in the shade of a large tree and digging. Nothing could have been more pleasurable than the surroundings; fruit and brilliant birds in the trees, richly carved buildings beneath the matted forest growths, the great plaza, 'studded with strangely carved monuments and surrounded by lofty mounds and great stone stairways, moss-grown and hoary with age, broken by the twisted roots of giant trees. . . . The huge mass of squared and faced building stones, the profusion of sculptured ornament, boldly carved human figures, strangely grotesque imps, half human and half animal. . . .' Much of this had been explored fifty years before by Stephens, but there remained dense scrub and thicket to be cleared. Maudslay dug into the great mounds and uncovered temples within them. Mrs Maudslay meanwhile kept house in the tent, doctored the villagers, watched the birds, for which she had a passion, acted as admiring spectator of the work in the plaza, and dreamt romantically of ancient Copan and its ways.

They went on to Quirigua, where the monuments were so thickly covered with vegetation that they looked like dead tree trunks; moss had to be scrubbed from the carvings, and sculptured monoliths disinterred from the roots of trees. A splendid altar was uncovered; rich doorways revealed; all about stood great mounds and terraces, with flights of stone steps. There were huge stone animals, with great trees growing from their backs; one, a turtle, carved all over with figures, weighed nearly twenty tons. Maudslay felled trees, cleared away earth, took photographs and mouldings in plaster and paper, some of the party got fever, and the work was broken off. Mrs Maudslay, more and more obsessed with animals, bought a baby squirrel; her great disappointment at Quirigua was that she did not see a monkey.

At Ixcun Maudslay discovered ruins of which no one knew; they were hidden under thick vegetation, and the site was impenetrable with wood and liana vine. He got twenty mozos working on them with machetes, and presently foundations of temples and houses, chambers, and sculptured monoliths appeared; an unimportant town of a good period. In some places there were no ruins visible, only conical mounds into which they dug, and, like magicians, resurrected a town. They proceeded over the Great Pine Ridge and down the Belize River into British Honduras, floated downstream on a raft, shot alligators, found an alligator's nest with thirty eggs, ate the eggs and shot the mother, reached Belize, and were soon off for the famous Chichen Itza, where, in 1842, Stephens and Catherwood had found a hacienda built among the ruins; forty years later Maudslay found the ancient city and the ruined hacienda covered in dense jungle. He engaged his workers and clearance began; he took up his residence in the Casa de Monjas, a fine Maya nunnery raised on a solid block of masonry and approached by a magnificent stairway; there was a broad terrace round the house, from which one looked over the vast rippling sea of the untouched forest.

To the north the ruins stretched, and the sunk, rock-walled lake which supplied the water, and the magnificent Castillo on its high stairwayed pyramid. Westward of the Castillo were colonnades and temples still unexcavated, and the great walled Ball Court, with its beautiful little tiger-friezed temple in one corner. Through the spring and summer Maudslay lived in the nunnery and worked at surveying, clearing, and making casts, in that 'ghostly grandeur and magnificence which becomes almost oppressive to one who wanders day after day amongst the ruined buildings'. Less fortunate in his lodging had been the French archaeologist, Désiré Charnay, who in 1881 made his headquarters in the open gallery of the Castillo, and found it exposed to a continual *courant d'air*. Nevertheless, M. Charnay fell under the spell of the dead city and its glorious surroundings, and spent much time evoking and musing on its extraordinary past. The Spanish had used the Castillo as a fortress; they had whitewashed over the reliefs of figures, which seemed to them irreligious; much time had to be spent in chipping away the whitewash. In its prime, Chichen Itza had been a great religious city of pilgrimages, temples and sacrifices; devout processions had wound through the forest to worship at its shrines five and six centuries ago. It has become so again. Processions still wind through those dense forests, processions of explorers, archaeologists, and their assistants, making pilgrimage and doing reverence to those carved gods that have risen again out of the green wilderness for our amaze, seeking for temples still buried and lost.

When they, the explorers, meet other explorers bound on the same quests, their ruin-pleasure may turn to bitterness, even to hate. Thus M. Charnay, camping on the river which divides Guatemala from Mexico and sighting a canoe rowed by white men:

'A horrible suspicion flashed across my mind that they were men belonging to another expedition, who had forestalled me. . . .'

Presently the canoe's owner was encountered among the ruins that M. Charnay was hoping to make his own.

'We were met by Don Alvaredo, whose fair looks and elastic step showed him to be an Englishman. We shook hands; he knew my name, he told me his: Alfred Maudslay, Esq., from London; and as my looks betrayed the inward annoyance I felt: "It's all right," he said, "there is no reason why you should look so distressed. My having had the start of you was a mere chance. . . . Come, I have had a place got ready; and as for the ruins, I make them over to you. You can name the town, claim to have discovered it, in fact, do what you please." '

So, owing to Mr Maudslay's magnanimity, all turned out well that time; M. Charnay explored the ruined place, named it Lorillard, and found it full of wonders – temples, palaces, richly sculptured lintels, idols. The neighbouring Lacandones had been used to performing their religious ceremonies in the ruins, until, a shy and diffident people, they had retired into the woods at the coming of white explorers. Mr Maudslay soon left Lorillard to the possessive Frenchman, and departed after other game. M. Charnay, a contentious man, had his own strongly held views on the dates, origins, times of abandonment, of all the Indian cities; most archaeologists are inclined to caution on these matters. . . .

The lost cities in the mountains of Peru were not the settlements of . . . wandering tribes, but the mountain fastnesses of the Inca chiefs, who built themselves eyries in the high sierras above the Cuzco valley and the basin of Titicaca, impregnable against their enemies and against the encroaching grasp of the invading Spaniards. So high and so steep their cities stood, so hidden in the forested, precipitous folds and canyons of the rocky sierras, that it has been possible to climb and walk the mountains about them for weeks and months and never come on them, until suddenly round the turn of a cliff a startling mass of stone towers on a plateau above a vertical jut of precipice. Such a lost city an American archaeologist, Mr Hiram Bingham, set out to seek some forty years ago; such a city he at last found, among the high peaks of Machu Picchu. He had read of it in Peruvian chronicles: the palace city built by the Inca Manco, fleeing from Pizarro's army, which had taken Cuzco, the Inca capital; this new royal city and shrine was hidden away in the inaccessibility of the great forested precipices.

'The royal city of Vilcapampa was completely lost. It was a sacred shrine hidden on the top of great precipices in a stupendous canyon, where the secret of its existence was safely buried for three centuries under the shadow of Machu Picchu mountain.'

Many expeditions had sought it in vain; its existence had been rumoured since 1875; it seemed untraceable and inaccessible. But Mr Bingham and his expedition traced it, setting out up the steep Urubamba valley, climbing past Inca ruins, passing a sugar plantation whose manager could not direct them, but who had heard it said that somewhere in the great forests there was an Inca city.

Then at last they came to the ruins of an Inca temple, standing by a dark, intimidating pool; this they took to be Vitcos. They pushed on through the great wild forest, climbing precipitous ravines and canyons, and always above them towered the snow-capped peaks. They came, after much mortal effort, to a small farm, where two Indians lived alone. From this place great green precipices fell away to the foaming rapids of the Urubamba below. Before them was a great granite cliff, two thousand feet high; thousands of feet above that rose the snowy mountains. Round a promontory was a great flight of beautifully made stone-faced terraces, which the Indians had lately cleared of forest. Following along one terrace into the uncleared forest beyond, they suddenly saw them, the Inca ruined houses, covered with the trees and moss of centuries; and, in the shadow of bamboo thickets and tangled vines, there rose walls of white granite ashlars beautifully fitted. Scrambling through the dense thickets, they came to a cave lined with cut stone – it seemed a royal mausoleum. Above it was a semi-circular building which reminded them of the temple of the sun in Cuzco; but it seemed to the delighted Mr Bingham even better than this Inca marvel, and as fine as any stonework in the world. 'It fairly took my breath away. What could this place be?' Near a clearing where the Indians had planted a small vegetable garden, stood two of the finest and most interesting structures in ancient America, built in Cyclopean blocks of beautiful white granite. They were roofless temples, twelve feet high.

Mr Bingham gazed with amaze on the beautifully constructed granite city, with its hundreds of terraces and stairs. Could this, he asked, be the principal city of Manco and his sons, that Vilcapampa where was the 'University of Idolatry' which the Spanish friars had tried in vain to reach? He photographed it, and they made a map.

Later, expeditions to Vilcapampa were organized; the site was cleared, roads made. The members of the expeditions were tough men; they climbed precipices, fell down them, tore the muscles of their arms, and never flagged in the desperate work. Now Vilcapampa is one of the great sights which draws South American tourists, who approach it by the new road. Four hundred kinds of bird have been found in the place, twenty snakes, ten lizards, and a variety of fishes. While naturalists pursued these creatures, Mr Bingham mused over his city's past.

'Surely this remarkable lost city which had made such a strong appeal to us on account of its striking beauty and the indescribable grandeur of its surroundings appears to have had a most interesting history.'

Mr Bingham was one of those explorers whose high romantic feeling seems to have lacked somewhat its adequate expression.

Machu Picchu, Peru. Terraces

102 Tikal, Guatemala. 'Structure 78'
This massive limestone stairway, its thirty-eight steps cleared now of the undergrowth, is still dwarfed by the towering trees. It is one of eighty or more lesser buildings which lie hidden at Tikal, each known now only by an archaeologist's number. Classic Tikal flourished, according to its own records, from AD 416 until 869. It was unknown to the outside world until 1696, when a Franciscan monk, Andrés de Avendaño, stumbled upon 'a number of ancient buildings which although they were very high and my strength very little, I climbed'.

103 Tikal, Guatemala. Temple I
This temple-pyramid in the Great Plaza of Tikal is now partially restored. To the top of its 'roof-comb' it towers 155 feet above the ground (the tallest temple IV is 229 feet high). The steep stairway of 100 steps is revealed, worn for centuries by the tread of priests and acolytes and, if these people were like their Aztec neighbours to the west, of human sacrifices who mounted only to tumble bleeding down again, leaving their torn-out hearts behind as an offering to the gods.

104 Tikal, Guatemala. Relief of a chieftain
Mayan art is ornate, alien, barbaric and often fear-inspiring. This man of rank is typical, with his elaborate head-dress of quetzal feathers, saucer-like ear ornaments, heavy necklace of shells and shield bearing the head of his protecting god. Something like 100 such monoliths have been discovered at Tikal.

105 Monte Alban, Mexico. Detail of a wall relief
A frieze of 140 life-size figures like these runs round the walls of the Temple of the Danzantes at Monte Alban, their strange distorted postures, open mouths and closed eyes suggesting that they represent the corpses of chiefs and kings slain in battle. Monte Alban, city of the gods, looks down from a treeless summit on to the Mexican town of Oaxaco. It has a known history dating from 500 BC until the coming of the Spaniards in AD 1519; the Temple of the Danzantes dates from its earliest phase.

106–7 Chichen Itza, Mexico. Columns from the Temple of the Warriors
The 'thousand columns' of Chichen Itza stretch five deep round the side of the Temple of the Warriors, from which this picture was taken, and four deep below its ceremonial stairway and along one side of the great plaza. They supported carved roof-beams of sapodilla wood. The temple was built about AD 1150, towards the end of the 'new age' of Chichen Itza, begun two centuries before when a defeated and exiled army—Toltecs from distant Tula, north of Mexico City—joined with the Mayan-speaking Itzas and settled in the tip of Yucatan. The columns bear the same martial motifs as those at Tula. Chichen Itza was re-discovered in its ruined and ghostly grandeur by John Lloyd Stephens and Frederick Catherwood in 1842.

108 Chichen Itza, Mexico. The Castillo
Four stairways of ninety-one steps run up the sides of this dominant pyramid at Chichen Itza, their balustrades decorated with plumed serpents, open-mouthed; the elaborate temple at the top carries the symbol of the sky-god, Quetzalcoatl. This view, from the Temple of the Warriors, looks across a stone figure representing the dreaded rain-god, Chac Mool, whose lap was levelled to receive the hearts of human sacrifices torn from the living body.

109 Chichen Itza, Mexico. Stairways
Since A. P. Maudslay and his workers took up residence at Chichen Itza in 1882, the massive trimmed and mortared stone has risen again from the dense jungle which covered the flat plain on which the city rests. These platform stairways still retain their ancient dignity.

110 Copan, Honduras. Demon from the 'Reviewing Stand'
One of these larger-than-life demonic figures, with its un-Mayan features, kneels at each end of the 'Reviewing Stand' at Copan. Serpents writhe from the corners of their mouths and are knotted round their waists; one hand holds a rattle or torch. The top step of the stand carries the date AD 771.

111 Machu Picchu, Peru. Trapezoidal doorway
The entrance to the fortress-sanctuary of Vilcapampa, high above the Andean valley of the river Urubamba, is unmistakably Inca. Its trapezoidal doorway, and the unmortared stones trimmed so closely to fit their fellows that a knife-blade, it is said, could not be inserted between them, are similar to those found in the Inca capital of Cuzco itself.
The vast empire of the Incas stretched down the west coast of South America for over 3000 miles, through desert, low-lying jungle and high mountains. Founded about AD 1100, it endured until its power was destroyed by the Spaniards in 1535. In the mountains the Incas built their famous chain of fortress-sanctuaries, and it was to one of these, Vilcapampa, that the Lord Inca Manco II fled from his Spanish masters. His new capital rested on a mountain saddle between two towering peaks, Machu and Huayna Picchu. To the east rose snow-capped mountains, on each side precipitous cliffs fell down to the valleys far below. It was a site secret and inaccessible, which needed no defences.

112 Tikal, Guatemala. Temple III
Now a seeming mound of rubble, this towering pile, 178 feet high, was once a precise and geometrical pyramid of trimmed and mortared masonry, surmounted by a temple of heavy stone. In the centuries since Tikal was deserted, the jungle has reasserted itself, and Nature's roots clutch deep between its once ordered stones; an old and haunted beauty remains. Eight of these mighty pyramids thrust their heads above the forest in the central square mile of Tikal.

113 Machu Picchu, Peru. View from the sanctuary
On the summit of the mountain saddle are the granite

remains of royal palaces, temples, sacred plazas and residential compounds for the soldiers and workmen. This view looks towards Huayna Picchu; hidden by the mists, the mountains rise beyond.

114 Machu Picchu, Peru. Terraces

The elaborate agricultural terraces, cleared now of the engulfing vegetation which overran them in the intervening centuries, are faced with close-packed stones which must have required great labour and constant repair. At the top stands a ruined temple, below graze llamas. During the Inca period llamas were regarded as state property and were bred by royal officials.

115 Copan, Honduras. Staircase to Temple XI

In the Great Court at Copan stood fourteen monumental stelae, intricately carved monoliths which are masterpieces of Mayan art. At the foot of the facing stairway stands stele N, with an altar in front made of a single stone in the form of a dragon. It is dated 9.16.10.0.0 (AD 761). The stairway, on which reconstruction has not yet begun, led up to Temple XI, at the south end of the Great Court of Copan. (See also p. 239)

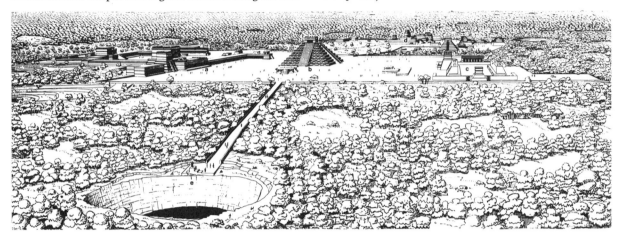

CHICHEN ITZA (above)
a Temple of the Warriors and 'Thousand Columns'
b The Castillo, with the 'Dance platform' before it
c Ball Court
d The Caracol or 'Observatory'
e Cenote or Sacrificial Well

COPAN (below)
a, b The Great Court with its many stelae
c Hieroglyphic Stairway
d Ball Court
e Jaguar Stairway to East Court of Acropolis
f Temple 11
g 'Reviewing Stand'
h Stele N
j Temple 22
k Stele C
In the background is the River Copan

113

III The haunting gods

BROKEN BEAUTY

The time-struck abbeys and ruinated churches of Europe, the broken, pillared temples, Doric, Ionic, Corinthian, that decorate the mountains and islands of Greece, greater Greece, Asia Minor, the Byzantine domes that climb the mountain-sides like figs, the mouldering mosques and fallen minarets, the great abbeys of Cyprus, the huge halls of Thebes, the drowned sanctuary of Philae, the shining grey pillars of Persia, the Assyrian, Roman and Oriental temples that stand beautifully about Mesopotamian deserts, the richly wrought, terraced, jungle-drowned palace-temples of Central and South America, of Burma and Ceylon, the Hindu and Mogul splendours of India, the eaved exquisites of China – all these are haunted by their gods, as the fallen palaces by their kings and courts, the streets of abandoned cities by the ghostly treading of feet, wrecked ports by the swish of keels in slipping waves, the clanking of anchors, the chaffering of merchants on the quays. It is not really possible to assess the various elements: the beauty, the ruination, the contrast of present desolation with former grandeur, the backcloth of some gorgeous or dim mysterious ancient past, the haunting of the gods. In Greece, perhaps, less possible than elsewhere, since the Greeks built their temples in places of the wildest beauty, and since their divine and secular history are so inextricably entangled together. Who can say, looking on Paestum, Segesta, Selinunte, Agrigentum, Delphi, Bassae, Aegina, the Temple of Zeus at Olympia, the mountain sanctuaries of Greek Asia Minor, what nerve is touched? . . .

All over Greece and her islands, Greek Asia Minor, Greece in Italy, the ruined temples stand. The most religious race in the world except the Jews (and more religious than the Jews, for they had many more gods, and therefore many more shrines), they built temples out of all proportion in number to their palaces, their castles, their triumphal arches, even their theatres. They stand about the mountains and valleys in their broken beauty, their classical perfection, haunted by their gods and by that uniquely magnificent past that is instilled into the mind of every literate child. That past is inescapable; it commands our spirits. Take it away, and what have we left? Finely proportioned buildings, usually in fine situations, in varying stages of ruin; the soul is gone.

Another question: what does ruin add to their beauty and to our emotion? If they stood today as they stood when first built, in all the glory of fresh paint, dazzling whiteness, polychrome sculptures, polished marble floors, roofs fraught with brightly hued godlike forms, should we admire them as much, or should we feel a faint suggestion of garishness, even of bad taste, in those brilliant, accomplished, flawless places of worship set so opulently in the barren mountain land above seas the vivid blue of posters? Now, mellowed, weathered, roofless and broken, their gay colour flaked away, half their columns prostrate on the ground around them, assaulted by the centuries, by enemies, by robbers, by the shaking of the earth, but still standing in their wrecked beauty among herbs and rocks and the encroaching wilderness, defying time, symbols of a lost civilization unparalleled in our history, they have achieved a unique emotional grandeur.

They are exquisitely foiled by the crumbling Byzantine churches that nestle like clustered fruits about the hills and valleys and cities of Greece. Too often in the undulant history of artistic taste, admiration for classical, Byzantine, Gothic or baroque architecture has been contemptuously exclusive, and visitors to Greece have exalted one mode of building to the detriment of others; actually the different styles set one another exquisitely off, each enhancing the beauties of its rivals, like contrasting colours and shapes in a flower bed. . . . Looking at the ruined Byzantine churches of Greece, Turkey and Asia, one compares the pleasure of these crumbling clustered Christian domes, often touchingly pretty and small, with that of the shattered glory of the Greek temples standing superbly on their olive-silver hills, or rock-strewn Sicilian forest slopes, or above the ruined shores of Tyrrhenian and Ionian bays; or with the more austere pleasures of the time-struck Gothic abbeys of western Europe; the charm of the broken Romanesque churches built into farmhouses and barns that stand among the fig-trees and olive-groves of Spain; of the broken baroque Cartujas that successive revolutions have shattered and that poverty and cynical apathy have left to moulder away; of the jungle-grown ancient temples of Mexico and the Maya country and Cambodia and Ceylon; the medieval Arab mosques that bear witness to the Islamic glories of Anatolia and of East Africa; the Assyrian temples lying buried, or piece by piece emerging, from under the medieval cities, villages and castles of Mesopotamia; all the uncountable broken places of worship that stand or lie like defeated prayers about the world. That air of defeat the ruined temples and churches all wear in common. One concludes, on the whole (perhaps this is a view purely personal), that classical temples gain by moderate breakage, but should not be entirely prone, and that their partial and skilful reconstruction is not amiss; that Byzantine churches are more exquisite when entire but a trifle decayed; that there is a quality peculiarly emotion-stirring in ruinous baroque, built for such graceful elegance and fallen on barbarous days. . . .

The sun god's temple at Bassae, high in the wild Arcadian mountains, calls for no restoration beyond the return of its frieze from the British Museum. The great statue of the god is gone, and might be replaced by one of the many now in galleries. The aesthetic impact of Bassae, standing in broken Doric splendour lost in wild hills, so solitary, so lost, that it remained unknown to any but local shepherds through centuries till it was discovered by chance in 1765 – the effect of Bassae is stupendous. To come on it unexpectedly on a mountain excursion, as the French architect did, must have been a ruin-pleasure unique in kind. . . . Bassae, designed by the architect of the Parthenon, set in its wild and lonely hills, has excited the passions of visitors ever since. . . .

The native island of Apollo and Artemis has lain, swinging at anchor in the eye of the sun, its sacred precincts for many centuries unexcavated, while history, once so active in and round it, passed it by. Today, though so little is to be seen of temples or monuments, except pedestals and sites, to walk among those to the high terrace where Apollo's temple stood, surrounded by what were treasuries, colonnades, courts and temples to other gods, has the excitement almost peculiar to the sanctuaries of Phoebus. Baedeker, with the fatuous inapprehensiveness that on occasion overtook this great man, remarks of Delos: 'The excursion is interesting only to archaeologists.' On the contrary: Delos is, of all places, calculated to capture the imaginations of those who do not know an exedra from a metope, Doric from Corinthian, and could not care less what columns in antis are. For here is the grotto where Apollo and Artemis were born; and I have seen a stout American lady galloping up the hillside to it, at full speed, calling to her daughter: 'Alice, Alice! Come and see the house where Apollo lived!' The cistus-grown, craggy island, so full of religious and secular history, with its sacred harbour silted up below it, its sanctuaries dominated by the high cone of Mount Kythnos, its barren, shrubbed, sweet-smelling solitude washed by the splashing or murmuring or tempest-driven sea, is poetry to the least informed. . . . Even more than at Delphi, a reconstruction of temples and statues is called for. Purists would be shocked; romantics deeply delighted. . . .

One would like, too, to see more going on in Ephesus. The great temple of Artemis . . . lost to view for so long, rediscovered eighty years ago, the site where successive temples had been built, each on the foundations of the temple before it, between the seventh century BC and Augustus, can never be built again; its gorgeousness was incomparable, and not for our drab days to emulate. It has been for the past half century a neatly laid-out site; so neat, so labelled, so tamed, that the goddess can scarcely haunt it. But in the grassy spaces of the great theatre, every full moon, the Ephesians might assemble in worship of their goddess, and shout for two hours, as they did two thousand years ago, when missionaries arrived with the message of an alien god, 'Great is Diana of the Ephesians.'. . .

Ephesus and the neighbouring Turkish village of Ayasoluk (at the foot of whose hill the Artemision had stood) were more picturesque before they were excavated; in the days when Wheeler and Pococke and Chandler and Hobhouse and Byron and Conybeare and Howson roamed about and found their own ruins, in the wild wide basin mountain-rimmed, golden with angelica and yellow iris, surrounded by mosques, wild rocks, and forest trees. . . . Gone are the days when Hobhouse and Byron put up their beds 'in a most miserable han' at Ayasoluk and partook of cold provisions on a stone seat by a fountain near a cypress-shaded mosque, and rambled about the ruins, climbing up to the Turkish castle and to the mosque built over Justinian's great church of St John, overrun with weeds and with shrubs shooting from the broken walls. A ruined minaret rose over the west door; a stork had made her nest in it; the broken columns of a portico stood in the court. Other ruined mosques stood near, the minarets of which might have been taken for the columns of some Grecian temple. The whole scene was desolate, and, said Hobhouse: 'cannot but suggest a train of melancholy reflections. The decay of three religions is there presented at one view. The marble spoils of the Grecian temple adorn the mouldering edifice once dedicated to the service of Christ, over which the tower of the Musselman is itself seen to totter and sink into the surrounding ruins.'

All the gods, in fact, had been, as usual, betrayed; but all the gods still haunt their broken temples.

120 Ephesus, Turkey. The statue of Scholasticia in the Baths
Scholasticia, whose statue this is thought to be, was a wealthy Christian lady who lived at the end of the fourth century AD. As a gift to her native city she improved and enlarged the public Baths, which were thereafter known as the Baths of Scholasticia.

121 Ephesus, Turkey. Statues in the Museum
The whole history of the Mediterranean world is stacked up here against the wall of Ephesus Museum. In the centre is one of several representations of the ancient Ephesian fertility goddess. Her own name is lost, but when the Greeks came they identified her with their own goddess of childbirth, Artemis; she was shown as a hieratic figure adorned with symbolic attributes—an elaborate necklace, rows of eggs (not, as was thought at one time, breasts) and below the waist animal-heads carved in threes. She is the image of fecund life. The Romans called her Diana, and St Paul caused a riot by preaching against her. Behind her, and on the left of the photograph, are two grave-slabs of gladiators, relics of the Romans who governed and amused themselves here for 500 years. The bearded head at the top may be the Egyptian corn-god Serapis, who had a shrine here. Other fragments show Graeco-Roman portrait busts and ornamental reliefs including the bull's head with the swag of fruit, seen in the Delos sculpture of Plate 124.

122 Paestum, Italy. The Temple of Poseidon
Were these columns once beneath the sea? A close examination of the one on the left shows that the bottom half seems far more deeply pitted and weathered than the top. The same 'tide-mark' occurs on all the columns of the Paestum temples and always at the same height—about 5 feet from the ground. More conclusive still, on the lower parts have been found the borings of a sea-mollusc called *lithodomus*, so that experts are now virtually certain that during the Middle Ages the sea-level rose, covering the low plain on which these fifth-century BC temples stand, and receded again to about its ancient level in the sixteenth and seventeenth centuries. It was a lucky freak of nature, for in this way three of the finest temples of the Greek world have been preserved almost intact. This detail from the 'Temple of Poseidon' (latest research suggests that it was in fact dedicated to Hera) looks past the inner row of columns towards the exterior row, with their sturdy fluted shafts, plain round capitals and flat abaci.

123 Ephesus, Turkey. A column from a colonnade
This combination of bull's head and Ionic capital is a vivid reminder of Ephesus' cosmopolitan background, for it unites in one aesthetic harmony the two great enemies of the ancient world—Greece and Persia. The bull capital is a typical and very common feature of Persian architecture down to the time of Darius and Xerxes; the Ionic column, though evolved first in the Greek cities of Asia Minor, is one of the most characteristic products of Greek art—subtle, elegant and strictly proportioned. This column has been reassembled by archaeologists and is not in its original position.

124 Delos. A column base
Long centuries of evolving art are summed up in the sculpture and architecture of the Hellenistic Age, of which this elaborate column base is typical. The use of bases with decoration in high relief comes from Asia Minor; the swags of fruit hanging from the bull's head (*bucranium*) is an ancient motif going back to Minoan times (second millennium BC) when an actual bull's skull was no doubt used; while the ornament along the top (called, for obvious reasons, 'egg and dart') belongs to the Archaic and Classical periods, appearing at its greatest refinement on such buildings as the Erechtheum.

125 Bassae, Greece. The Temple of Apollo Epicurius
Still well preserved after nearly 2500 years, the Doric temple at Bassae (seen here from the west) stands far from any town. It is built of grey limestone (not, like the Parthenon, of marble) and marks the fulfilment of a vow by the little state of Phigalia for deliverance from the plague in the mid-fifth century BC. It is unusual in several ways, including the first use in architecture of the Corinthian capital, on one single column of the interior.

126 Ephesus, Turkey. The Marmorean Way
Paved with marble, well-drained and lined with monuments, fountains and stone benches, the 'Via Marmorea' (Marble Road) must once have been an imposing and beautiful thoroughfare. It was planned by Alexander the Great's general Lysimachus, who rebuilt Ephesus two miles from its former site (which was sinking into a swamp: its proudest possession, the Temple of Artemis, is now 30 feet below ground level). The Romans added to it, making it yet more splendid, but by the Middle Ages Ephesus had crumbled to a mere village.

127 New Paphos, Cyprus. Detail of a floor in the House of Mosaics
This was the floor of a rich Roman's house at the end of the third century AD. More than fourteen of the rooms in the villa, which was discovered only in 1962, were inlaid with this costly mosaic-work, showing animals, human figures, hunting scenes and mythological subjects. The purely ornamental motifs are of great delicacy and charm. This detail includes interlocking crescents and (below) arabesque foliage patterns with a tiny bird in the centre, cleverly brought to life with a few *tesserae*.

128 Didyme, Turkey. A Medusa mask from the Temple of Apollo
From the high frieze that ran above the columns of the Temple at Didyme a row of Medusa heads like this looked down, the last descendants of those protecting demons that had glared forth from the pediments of Archaic temples 800 years before. By AD 200 they have become humanized and approachable, suffering rather than inspiring terror. The writhing hair, pursed mouth, fixed gaze and deeply furrowed brow betray the anguished emotion of Hellenistic art. This slab of stone has now fallen and lies among the débris of the once great shrine of Apollo.

129 Leptis Magna, Libya. Columns from a portico

This colonnade, originally crowned with arches, is one side of a courtyard behind the theatre, apparently a sort of 'foyer' for the wealthy members of the audience to walk, meet and shelter from bad weather. It is part of the large-scale extensions to Leptis Magna carried out under Septimius Severus (who was born here) and Hadrian. The granite columns carry finely carved Corinthian capitals of East Mediterranean type.

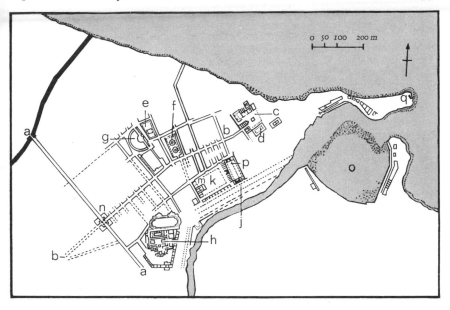

LEPTIS MAGNA
a,a Decumanus (main east–west street)
b,b Cardo (main north–south street)
c   Old Forum
d   Old Basilica
e   Portico behind Theatre
f   Market
g   Theatre
h   Hadrianic Baths
j   Colonnaded street
k   Severan Forum
m   Temple
n   Four-way Triumphal Arch
o   Harbour (silted up)
p   New Basilica

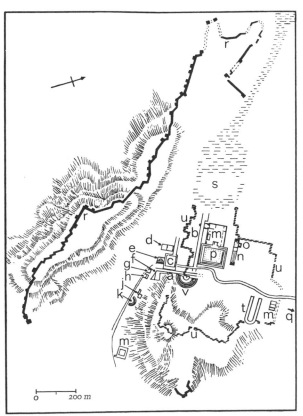

EPHESUS
a   Mamorean Way
b   Arcadian Way
c   Agora
d   Temple of Serapis
e   Library of Celsus
f   Baths of Scholasticia
g   Temple of Hadrian
h   Fountain
j   Town Hall
k   Odeion
m   Gymnasia
n   Twin Churches of St Mary
o   Baptistry
p   Verulanus Hall
q   To Temple of Artemis (2 miles)
r   Greek walls
s   Old Harbour (now marsh)
t   Stadium
u   Byzantine walls
v   Theatre

FALLEN SHRINES

The grandeur of the vanished abbey haunts the lonely site. . . . Here princes came, and bards, here wars and sieges raged, here are the graves of poets and great chiefs. Today the curlews cry over the wild bog-lands . . . and if you turn up the earth among the ruins you may come on some fragments of broken medieval tile. . . .

The sixteenth century thundered in . . . and in Britain abbeys and monasteries fell like broken trees beneath the brutal axe, and stood in shattered, decaying magnificence to haunt men's souls. The Dissolution did much to add the dimension of ruin to British life; a half-superstitious reverence and awe surrounded and englamoured those fallen, tree-grown shrines that silently (unless they were appropriated for mansions) went more to earth as the seasons passed over their roofless frames and sprouting aisles where the encircling woods pressed in and foxes made their lairs. The melancholy beauty of ruins as such sank deeply into the human mind. . . .

How soon after the destruction of the abbeys did this melancholy pleasure in their ruined grandeur and pathos begin? Some, of course, were taken over at once, with less or more of adaptation, for private mansions, most decayed gradually into ruin, serving as quarries for builders; parts of them were incorporated into farms and barns; many stood broken and mouldering away for all to gaze on. . . .

Looking on Bellum Locum, on Tintern, on Glastonbury, those majestic shells of splendour and grace, on Rievaulx lying magnificent in its broad glen under steep green terraced cliffs, on Fountains striding across its river, on Kirkstall, demeaned into the pleasure park of a hideous Leeds suburb, on the desolation of Whitby, disintegrating in the wild salt winds on its high cliff between moor and sea – looking on these, and on the ruins of all the lost abbeys and priories that once so richly bejewelled Britain, one is moved to rage; the rage, only more bitter and personal, that assaults the mind at the sight of the churches and monasteries of Spain destroyed in periodic fits of Iberian anti-clerical fury. The destruction of the British abbeys was a crime for which there was not even that excuse; cold greed and rapacity are motives less respectable. . . .

As the memory of the living monasteries faded, and a generation grew up which had never known them but as shattered piles of lost magnificence, the homes of bats, owls, ghosts, and the homeless poor, they must have been regarded with a certain eerie dread; for one who, like the Gothic soldier, strayed from his troops 'to gaze upon a ruinous monastery', there must have been hundreds who preferred to give the doubtless haunted piles a wide berth, not knowing what dubious shapes and shades might emerge from those wrecked gateways and broken cloisters. Some might have been taught that the monkish inhabitants were a good riddance, having led lives not only of sloth and superstition, but of the greatest immorality; others would have mourned them as holy men and sources of charity to the poor, and anyhow as part of the immemorial British scene and way of life. . . . What lives were led by individual monks matters little; like lives led elsewhere, they were, no doubt, mixed. What matters is the enshrining of an idea, the splendour and incomparable grace of the buildings, the libraries, the manuscripts, the fishponds, the vineyards, the grange barns, the ordered beauty of the religious services, the hospitality, the charity at the gates, the great bells that pealed over the countryside.

It would have been possible, in our past centuries of wealth, to have restored and rehabilitated many of the abbeys; to have filled them again with communities, of one sex or another, of one or another branch of the Christian Church (it matters little which; they might be shared out, Anglicans to get most) and to have converted others into cathedrals or churches. It is not possible now; we are a ruined nation; the time may (improbably) come again, when we can afford such exquisite expenditure by ceasing to spend our all on weapons, so brittle and barbarous, of war. Losing the beauty of ruin, we should regain that of abbeys; a few ruins – perhaps Netley, Rievaulx, Glastonbury, Beaulieu, Fountains, and those which have been irrevocably and beautifully merged in secular houses – might be kept as they are, to satisfy our appetite for ruinous beauty. . . .

The tremendousness of Fountains, flung across its smooth river, with its complex jumble of periods, stuns the imagination with magnificence; Rievaulx, too, even more actually beautiful in situation, lying in the bend of a deep river valley, beneath climbing terraces cut in the precipitous hill, and fronted with steep woods. These two great Cistercian ruins rival each other in grandeur. Fountains has the charm of rising in its ruined splendour from smooth, charming, artificially laid out pleasure grounds, constructed in 1720 to surround the abbey, with every device of their style and period except artificial ruins; who could forbear not to use such heaven-given actual ruins as a centre for the landscape garden? To lay it out was a delicious pleasure, increased no doubt by the handsome Jacobean mansion that had been erected in 1611 in the abbey grounds. A huge thirteenth-century ruined abbey; an old-world mansion; a planned landscape park; the ensemble was, and is, both elegant and sublime.

Rievaulx's stance is even finer. The abbey itself has been left to progressive decay; it belonged to the first Duke of Buckingham, whose castle of Helmsley is near by. The second duke sold the abbey and grounds to Sir Charles Duncombe; it was his nephew who saw their capabilities (as Brown would have put it) as a landscape, and cut the fine terrace on the hill that rises sheer above the glen, building a circular temple at one end of the high ridge, and an elegant pavilion, adorned with paintings, at the other. From the temple one has a superb view of the abbey, standing far below. The landscape is completed by the handsome Vanbrugh mansion, Duncombe Park. In the middle of all the eighteenth-century elegance, the great thirteenth-century ruin moulders, grass-grown and tree-grown, the Gothic romance of those who gazed down on it from the belvedere on the high ridge.

> *Ah then most happy, if thy vale below*
> *Wash, with the crystal coolness of its rills,*
> *Some mould'ring abbey's ivy-vested wall,*

as one of the greatest of landscape gardeners ejaculated. Indeed, it seems odd that still more ruined abbeys have not been made the centres of planned landscapes, since an ecclesiastical touch has always been held to improve a gentleman's park, and some have set up on their estates ancient arches from some ruined church, and even a font, to add a Christian note among classical porticoes and groves of trees. . . .

In the case of Fountains, when the question of restoration and rehabilitation was recently raised, the mind is divided. Do we wish these dead stones to live, soaring into the skies, pealing with bells, summoning to prayer, humming with religion instead of bees, sweet with incense instead of wild flowers, dispensing charity at the gates, affording shelter to travellers, lives of piety to their inmates? So far so good: but there is no doubt that the shape and picturesqueness of the buildings would be greatly spoilt, as can be seen in nearly all the reconstructed and restored churches and monastic buildings of Europe. . . . On the whole, fine ruins should not be restored unless their use is necessary: they are part of the aesthetic kingdom of the eye and mind; like the poetry and painting of desolation. . . .

Our ruined abbeys and churches are, as a rule, only too well tidied up and cleared, losing in the process who can say how much of mystery and nostalgic awe. Many were built up long since into manor houses or farmhouses or barns, so that one may see chancel arches and fragments of carved stone and Gothic windows in the most incongruous places, in a thousand farm buildings standing about the countryside. . . . But this is among the ordinary vicissitudes of English abbeys, nearly all of which have contributed less or more to neighbouring buildings; all over the country manor houses, farms and cottages are haunted with strange intimations from shadowy vanished worlds; long refectories are piled with hay and strewn with agricultural tools, and in cow-house walls are niches where once saints stood.

But, when too much ruined to be tidied up, still the foundations and fragments of the great abbeys lie neglected in fields and commons, among thrusting woods and trees. . . . The ancient church in the woods . . . has fallen into dilapidated sanctity, hallowed and haunted; Christ among the dryads and fauns of the coppice that pushes round it. . . .

Solemnity . . . is certainly increased by surrounding woods. 'The pointed ruin peeping o'er the wood' is less commonly observed today than once it was. But here and there one finds, in the heart of a dark and shadowy thicket, such ruins as those of Bindon Abbey, the twelfth-century Cistercian monastery near Lulworth; fragments of wall, a few bases of columns, indications of the cloister court and refectory, everything grown with ivy and becoming one with the devouring woods. Round the abbey lie dark, shadowed fishponds. The monastery was pulled down at the Dissolution, 'A faire monasterie of White Cistercian monks', wrote the antiquarian Dorset parson Mr Coker a few years later; and 'out of the Ruines that faire house which stands there' (Lulworth Castle?) was raised by Viscount Bindon, a Howard, who should have kept better faith with his church. What he left was quarried away for later buildings: it probably supplied the Jacobean parts of the old manor house at Wool, where the Angel Clares honeymooned, and the barn with its ecclesiastical Gothic details. Bindon's utter desolation and mournful bosky twilight, through which the perceptive are aware of rambling, breviary-reading, or angling monks, have deepened century by century. . . .

Celtic ruins, usually in a wilder setting, wear another look. Ireland, that land of ecclesiastical and other ruins, is strewn every few miles with abbeys (mostly Anglo-Norman of the twelfth and thirteenth centuries, smaller, on the whole, than the English abbeys, and less fine in architecture), Franciscan friaries, and fifth-, sixth- and seventh-century Celtic oratories and churches. These oratories and monastic buildings, small, solid, often beehive-shaped, founded by the Irish missionary saints, often escaped wrecking by the Danish pirates owing to their inaccessibility, built on rocky islands off the west coast or in lonely lakes, or on mountain-tops, they need resolute seeking. In these lonely, wild resorts, the early missionaries made their centres among sea birds and rocks; to reach St Finan's monastery on the Great Skellig rock, one crosses seven and a half miles of uneasy sea and climbs six hundred steps. Pilgrims have done penance by climbing the highest rock peak, above the ruined oratories and cells. It is this kind of setting that gives the early Celtic monasteries their peculiar, intimidating fascination. Most of the oratories and churches are tiny, desolate, remote: one remembers that from these hut-like monastery cells Christianity radiated over Europe, as well as from the centres of light and learning in the plains – St Columba's Kells, wrecked by the Danes, Clonfert on the Shannon, with its cathedral that succeeded Brendan's monastery, Clonmacnoise, that huddle of crumbling chapels and belfries, gravestones and crosses, to which Alcuin and Charlemagne did honour, and which founded houses in Europe that still live, St Kevin's Glendalough, desolate between mountains and lake, that miraculous group of buildings behind its gateway – a hermit's cell that grew into a monastery, into a college, into a town; Dane-destroyed, it keeps its ruined cathedral, its little ruined churches, its high bell-tower, the two-storeyed oratory; at week-ends it is dense with visitors. Of late years it has been furbished up, the cathedral restored, the Round Tower re-capped, little St Saviour's Priory built up into neatness; it no doubt looked better before; about a hundred and twenty years ago Mr and Mrs Hall wrote of St Saviour's that only two of its sculptured pillars were in good condition, the ruin being overgrown with brambles, and a mountain ash growing through a wall; their illustration shows a ruin indeed. They found Glendalough very gloomy and delightful. . . .

> A weight of awe, not easy to be borne,
> Fell suddenly upon our spirit – cast
> From the dread bosom of the unknown past. . . .

Now visitors throng Glendalough to admire, and to enjoy that 'weight of awe' from the past, and the beauty of the ruinous vestiges . . . of five hundred years of monastic culture.

Cashel, too, is tourist-beset. The famous Rock towers precipitate over the shabby little town and the rich, treeless, mountain-bounded vale of Tipperary; the ruined thirteenth-century cathedral stands like a fort, a Gothic mass of stone, roofless and collapsed, a high round tower by its north transept, a castle in its west end, ruins of abbeys and walls lying round it, the beautiful little twelfth-century Cormac's Chapel nestling against its south wall. There, in this small corbel-roofed, arcaded-walled chapel, is Irish Romanesque, that fleeting lovely decoration that the Anglo-Norman invasion was to check, at its richest and most beautiful. The carved, zigzagged round entrance porch suggests in its exuberance a chaster Manueline. Visitors complain that both the chapel and the cathedral were more romantic when they stood wholly ruinous among their old walls and abbey remains and nettles and weeds and piles of boulders; now they are rescued from decay, tidied up, pieced together, thronged about with week-end admirers, and preserved by the Ministry of Works. Even so, their beauty staggers and disturbs.

Like other Irish ecclesiastical ruins and restorations, like Jerpoint Abbey, like Graiguenamanagh, both Cistercian (the latter disagreeably restored and vulgarized, but still the remains of the great walls of the English abbey of Duiske rove round the little town in strange sadness) . . . Cashel weighs on us with melancholy. This Irish melancholy – one can feel it in Kilkenny, the one-time capital of the English Pale, with its shattered old cathedral, its smart new one, its ruined abbeys and friaries along the Nore, its English-town and Irish-town, its alleys and lanes, where Gothic doorways and carved pillars support mean houses, its memories of the Kilkenny Statute that put the Irish in their place in the fourteenth century, of the parliament of Confederate Catholics of 1642, of Cromwell's siege of 1650, that smashed up the cathedral and its glass. Now Kilkenny has gone native again; the 'mere Irish' are in possession; the descendants of the Pale could repeat in their own sense the Gaelic lament for the dispossessed MacCarthy lords of Killarney

> The heart within my breast this night is wild with
>   grief
> Because of all the haughty men who ruled this place
> From Cashel and from Thomond to the wave beneath
> None lives, and where they lived lives now an alien
>   race.

But it is the dispossession of the ancient Catholic glory of Ireland that gives Irish church and monastic ruins their grief. Here once was a Church that travelled the world, mixing on equal terms with the great Churches of Europe, intellectually at one with the great scholastic foundations of France, Germany,

Italy, Britain, founding Continental daughter-houses, peopling them with Irish monks, conversing at Charlemagne's court, illuminating manuscripts and writing poems, inventing its own architecture, building abbeys that held towns within their walls – here, its exquisite broken ruins behind us, was such a Church once. Among the ruins now rise the brash modern chapels and churches that represent the Irish Church today, bemeaned and deflowered by the bitter centuries of persecution which, though they could not crush it out of existence, plucked from it the proud flower of its intellect and breeding, reducing it to a devout provincialism. It is a fact that one cannot travel more than a few miles in Ireland without passing some broken abbey or church; they lie strewn along coast and river, hill and plain, island and lake-side, in ruinous profusion. Destroyed by Danes, by Normans, by Englishmen, by decay, by time, by poverty, vandalism and dissolution, their crumbling arches and portals and fragments of wall stand in reproachful witness to the passing of a murdered culture. . . .

'Amidst the gloom arose the ruins of the abbey, tinged with a bright ray, which discovered a profusion of rich Gothic workmanship; and exhibited in pleasing contrast the grey stone of which the ruins are composed, with the feathering foliage that floated round them. . . . The imagination formed it, after the vision vanished.'

'The imagination formed it'; that is the constant and eternal element, behind all the pleasures supplied by architecture, associations, history, the grandeur of the monastic past, its superstitions, vices and corruptions, moral satisfaction over its destruction, religious lamentations over the same, investigation into the several strata of building, comparison of Benedictine, Cistercian, Augustinian, Carthusian, Premonstratensian, indignation, awe, ghosts, screech-owls, vespers whispered down the wind, the protestant view, the catholic view, the antiquarian view, the common sightseer's view of these marvels of the past (compare the Frankish awe of the ancient Greek buildings among which they settled and reared their castles – those ruins were obviously the work of *'les géants'* of some dim past, to be reverenced with half superstitious astonishment and uneasiness). But beneath all these feelings, a constant sentiment was pleasure in picturesque beauty. Dorothy Wordsworth at Rievaulx – 'Green grown hillocks among the ruins . . . wild roses. I could have stayed in this solemn quiet spot till evening . . .', and at Dryburgh – 'a very sweet ruin, standing so enclosed in wood. . . .'

So we have all felt and feel. . . . A good setting is, to the average ruin-seer, a good deal more important than interesting architecture; these need some background of knowledge; the pleasures of picturesque setting, only a simple sense of beauty. . . . Elgin Cathedral and Dryburgh add to splendour of architecture the romance of forest setting. . . . The beauty of Melrose is largely in its rich architectural detail, and, as in all the Scottish abbeys . . . (assaulted in war by the enemy neighbour, in religious disapproval by Caledonian reformers, mutilated and deformed into Presbyterian kirks, bickered over by the local lairds, who quarrelled unceasingly and tartly for places for their burial and pews for their worship, built about with ugly houses and shops, falling gradually into decay) . . . in the succession of one style on another, from Norman to perpendicular. . . .

After Mr Knox had done his job, the forlorn abbeys became a prey to squatters, to quarriers, to citizens who divided the buildings and lands among themselves, and kept part of the church for a kirk. Shops, houses and mean streets sprang up round the great walls.

'Instead of lonely ruins hidden in shielding forests, forgotten often of man, we find the glories of ancient Scotland jostled by taverns, workshops and inns, rising sheer, not from green meadows or amongst tangled thickets of thorns, but out of unseemly assemblages of shops and houses crowding up into cloister and graveyard, obliterating every trace of chapter house, refectory, dorter, even in some cases of portions of the church itself.'

It would seem that, of the great Scottish ecclesiastical ruins, only Elgin and Dryburgh, standing among their woods, have been preserved from this squalid entourage. Yet there is dramatic pleasure in the towering beauty of Jedburgh, for instance, rising unexpectedly and improbably from its crowded surroundings, rather as the Forum of Trajan used to from huddled streets, striking the eye with amaze. Melrose is less wholly surrounded, less sudden, can be approached on two sides from open space; but it too has the effect of a noble incongruity, apart from its rich poetic and pictorial elaboration of beauty.

In Wales, too, church and abbey ruins abound. They always have. All through the Middle Ages the Welsh ecclesiastical foundations suffered rapine and assault; every Norman and English raid, every rebellion and its suppression, every baronial disturbance, every outbreak of Owen Glendower, left in its wake a trail of smashed and plundered churches and monastic buildings. The royal ruffians in turn took their will of them; the Edwards, Richards, Henrys and their agents looted and sacked; when the last Henry had his turn, the abbeys he dissolved and spoiled were many of them already in ruin, their revenues given away to English colleges. The native population disliked them as foreigners, as rich, as reputedly immoral, as pets of Rome (for they claimed exemption from episcopal authority and to be subject to the Pope alone), above all, as bad neighbours, robbing the land from its owners, the tithes from the local parish priests, the very churches themselves. . . . If we are to believe contemporary comments, all monastic orders began well and soon declined. Whatever their moral errors, the Cistercians set their glorious houses beautifully about the wild glens and hills of Wales, often choosing sanctuaries already long hallowed by Celtic monastic cells. Still the ruins gape about the glens and hills; Tintern, Valle Crucis, Strata Florida, Cwmhir, Margam, Neath, Whitland; others wholly gone to earth. Tintern has, one supposes, given as much high poetic pleasure to ruin-gazers as even the finest English abbeys. Valle Crucis, too; there is more of it than of any other abbey in north Wales, and its position above the Dee is magnificent. As to Strata Florida, once 'the Westminster Abbey of Wales', with a church larger than St David's Cathedral, with its granges scattered over many acres, there is little left but the west portal, two ruined small buildings, and some fourteenth-century tiles. . . .

It would have been pleasant to see Llandaff Cathedral two hundred years ago, when Pococke visited it. It had decayed into ruin during two centuries of neglect and robbery. . . . All this was tidied up in the middle of the nineteenth century, when the cathedral was at last restored. . . . Llandaff is picturesque no more. In 1941 it became a bomb-ruin, it is now being repaired. Its bombed, roofless state induces comparisons. These modern war ruins have an air of painful futility that stirs anger; an anger less often roused by the no less criminal and futile catastrophes of the past. The destructive bestiality was the same; but usually the long years, the swathing ivy and the thrusting trees, the extreme beauty which the conditions of ruin can create, muffle the anger and the vexation. But the haunting gods hover about with reproachful sighs: one cannot forget.

In Wales particularly one feels disgust, turning from the lovely vestiges of greatness to what has replaced them: the mean, brash little conventicles that spatter the wild countryside with their ugliness. Most are dissenting chapels; some are Roman Catholic; in appearance there is little to choose. The Anglican churches are usually better, because older. But what must Wales have looked like with abbeys and priories, their granges and monastic buildings, rising in glens and valleys, on mountain and river side, all about its land? Hugh Latimer begged that a few religious houses might be left in each shire, 'not in monkery, but so as to be converted to preaching, study and prayer'; but, since Henry's aim was neither to destroy monkery nor to encourage preaching, study and prayer, this would have seemed to him silly. It is an agreeable fancy, communities of clerkly scholars studying the reformed religion and the new learning in the libraries, halls and cloisters of Valle Crucis, Tintern and Strata Florida, dispensing the sacraments according to the reformed rite at their ancient altars, emerging to preach the word to their wild flocks on those wild hills.

Rievaulx Abbey, Yorkshire. Ruined presbytery

138 Rievaulx Abbey, Yorkshire, England

Seen from a hill against which it is set, the Cistercian abbey of Rievaulx is framed by woods and fields—isolation which the monks who founded it in 1131 deliberately chose so that they could live undisturbed in self-contained communities. This view looks down across the remains of the thirteenth-century presbytery (flanked by the graceful skeletons of two flying buttresses). Beyond that, and at right angles to it, is the monks' refectory. A long Norman nave stretched away behind the trees to the right.

The Cistercians, for a time the most important monastic order in medieval England, began in 1098 when a group of monks led by an Englishman called Stephen Harding broke away from the abbey of Molesme in Burgundy and built a wooden church in the forest of Citeaux (Cistercium). Their purpose was to return to the strict Rule of St Benedict, the observance of which, after five centuries, was becoming very lax. Their reforming zeal soon spread throughout Europe and took root in England after 1128, especially in the wild and rugged country of the Scottish and Welsh borders and the moorlands of Yorkshire. Rievaulx was founded in 1131; Tintern Abbey in the same year; Fountains in 1132; Melrose, a daughter house of Rievaulx, in 1136; Bindon in 1172; Valle Crucis in 1201. By the 1160s Rievaulx had over 700 people living in it, so that, as an old chronicle says, 'the church swarmed with them, like a hive with bees'.

139 Bindon Abbey, Dorset, England

Only a few crumbling walls mark the site of Bindon Abbey. But its foundations—which can still be clearly traced—are notable: not altered or added to since the twelfth century, they preserve intact the original standard layout used in the early Cistercian abbeys: the cloister against the nave, dormitory and chapter-house on the east and frater (refectory) on the south.

140 Rievaulx Abbey, Yorkshire, England

Seen from a gap in the wall of the lay-brothers' range. In the foreground is the cloister, with part of the arcade of small round arches on twin stone shafts still standing. Higher up, against the sky, is the great arch of the crossing (with two small eye-like windows which can be located in Plate 138, just at the edge of the obscuring trees). Beyond this and below, the many-arched interior of the presbytery.

141 Fountains Abbey, Yorkshire, England

Built partly out into the river Skell, Fountains was one of the largest, and is still one of the best preserved of the Cistercian monasteries. Symmetrically framed in the dark arch of an old bridge over the river, the nave with its wide arched window is visible at the left, while leading out from it to the right stretches the long low frame of what was once the lay-brothers' dormitory. Beyond both is a massive, 170-foot tower, put up—in defiance of the early Cistercian strictures against excessive ornament or display—by an early sixteenth-century abbot named Huby.

142–3 Cashel Rock, County Tipperary, Eire

'Cashel of the Kings' ('Cashel' means fortified place) is one of the most storied sites in all Ireland. For on this barren hill once stood the ancient Irish capital of Munster—a combined fortress, palace and monastery (some parts of it—the Round Tower and Cormac's Chapel—go back to this time). In 1169 King Donall piously donated the whole outcropping to the church, and the cathedral whose ruins are still there was finally completed in the thirteenth century. Characteristically, however, its history was to be far from tranquil. In the foreground is part of Hore Abbey, originally a Benedictine monastery, but abruptly taken from that Order and handed over to the Cistercians in 1272 by the then Archbishop. The Archbishop did it, as he himself explained with disarming logic, because he had 'dreamed that the Benedictines had made an attempt to cut off his head'. This ecclesiastical excuse might have stood as the last word on trouble-making—around Cashel Rock, at least—had not Gerald, Earl of Kildare in 1495, decided to burn down the cathedral during a quarrel between himself and the Archbishop of Cashel. Called upon by the King to excuse this outrageous act afterwards, the Earl explained, 'I thought the Archbishop was inside'.

144 Great Skellig, Eire, St Finan's monastery

About seven miles out in the Atlantic, off the stormy coast of County Kerry, lies a group of small rocky islands which rise sheer out of the sea. On one of them, Great Skellig, these jagged steps, desolate piles of rubble wall, and an old weathered gravestone of the seventh century mark the site of one of the earliest centres of the great Celtic church which for a time was the only form of Christianity in Britain. St Finan's monastery was founded by some of the first Christians to journey (in the fifth and sixth centuries) to the land lying outside the bounds of the Roman Empire—a band of hermits and missionaries who probably sought out the inaccessible spot (it is more than 500 feet up from the water) for protection. They went out in small boats to preach in Ireland and Scotland, died as martyrs often as not and sometimes were buried in the cemetery that huddled beside their huts on the windy rock. Today a visitor hardy enough to climb the 620 steps cut in the sheet cliff-face and so reach the ruins can see the remains of six 'beehive' stone cells with overlapping stone roofs and a hole in the middle for smoke where these early Christians lived. In addition there are two primitive 'oratories', a few wells, some ancient crosses over equally ancient graves and a church built centuries later. Little Skellig, another island, can be seen in the distance.

145 Dryburgh Abbey, Berwickshire, Scotland

Along the valley of the Tweed, the shattered walls of Dryburgh Abbey lie open to the touch of sun and weather. The monks who had the abbey built and consecrated were Premonstratensians, an Order founded in 1120 at Prémontré in northern France. Today parts of the church and cloister are left, together with the foundations and gabled ends of the canons' frater, originally lit by four tall windows on the now open side and by the beautiful wheel-window in the west gable (shown here). The kitchen lay through the door at the far end under the wheel-window.

146 Melrose Abbey, Roxburghshire, Scotland
In 1136 a band of monks from Rievaulx who had come north at the invitation of David I, King of Scots, founded and began building the Abbey of Melrose in the exquisitely beautiful countryside of the Tweed Valley. But in the fourteenth century invading English armies twice pillaged and burnt it and the church was virtually rebuilt. The great window of the south transept (shown here) is English curvilinear tracery at its loveliest.

147 Tintern Abbey, Monmouthshire, England
Seen from the floor of the presbytery, looking westward. Tintern is most famous for its setting in the deep wooded hills of the Wye Valley, the inspiration for William Wordsworth's great poem. Although the remains now

standing date from the thirteenth century, Tintern Abbey began much earlier, in the 1130s with the first great wave of Cistercian building.

148 Cashel Rock, County Tipperary, Eire
The Round Tower and ruined nave of Cashel Cathedral stand out against a darkening sky. The graveyard crosses, Celtic in type, are modern.

149 Valle Crucis Abbey, Denbighshire, Wales
Cistercian records tell the exact date of the founding of Valle Crucis—28 January 1201. But no one knows exactly what events transformed it from a flourishing, if small, monastery into the dark and looming ruin that it is today. Most of the west front, seen in this picture from what was once the inside of the abbey, was built in the thirteenth century, but the small rose window was cut later. Over it a Latin inscription is still legible. Translated it reads: 'Abbot Adam carried out this work. May he rest in peace. Amen.'

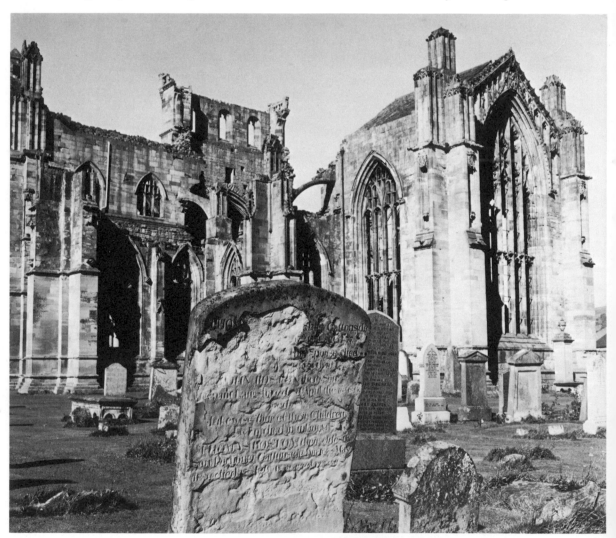

Melrose Abbey, Roxburghshire, Scotland

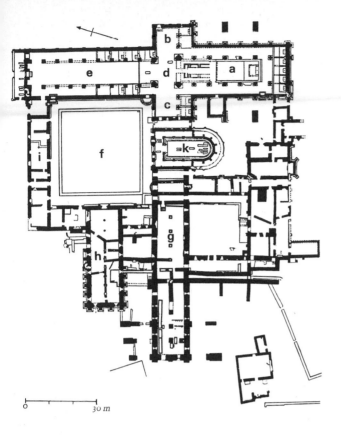

RIEVAULX ABBEY

RIEVAULX AND
FOUNTAINS ABBEYS
a Presbytery
b North transept
c South transept
d Crossing
e Nave
f Cloister
g Monks' dormitory (upper
   floor)
h Frater
j Lay-brothers' dormitory
k Chapter-house
l Tower

0   30 m

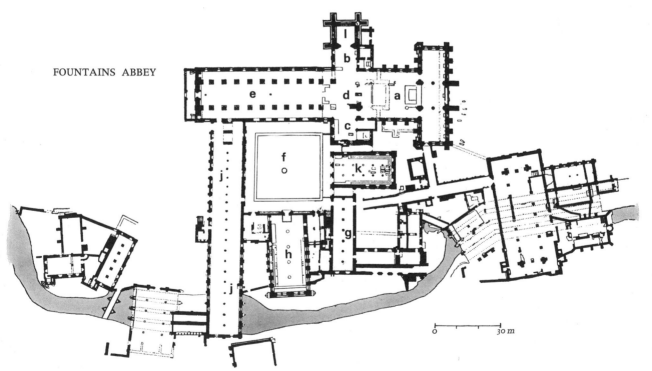

FOUNTAINS ABBEY

0   30 m

THE GREEN DUSK

The barbaric temples of the jungles need no ruining to enhance their mysterious awe, though an extra intensity of delight is given by the thrust of trees through roof and walls. In fact, enjungled ruins, religious or secular, are in a class apart. There are few now in Europe; one does not now have the excitement of pushing through the Kentish weald or a Devonshire combe or the Forest of Arden or the great wild woods of Roncevalles or the Black Forest of Bavaria or the woody crags of the Apennines where Romans chased the boar, and finding in the heart of dense jungle some lost forgotten city, or tree-grown palace, or broken temple with boughs pushing greenly through window, door and roof. True, the boughs push and the shrubs grow and the creepers sprawl across smashed altars in modern cities now; but these derelict shattered relics stand in the open for all to see; no jungle swallows them into its green dusk. . . .

Turn from the Mediterranean, the Ionian and Aegean seas, the clear, naked atmosphere of Europe, of Syria, of Asia Minor, the great temples standing in their shattered glory on pine-clad mountains, or buried in rocky valleys, or shining palely against golden deserts, or in Gothic grace among British and French landscapes, haunted by the gods of our Greek and Oriental cults; turn to the green dusk. Buried in deep jungles lie the hidden or discovered temples of the east and the west; Ceylon, Java, Burma, parts of India, the great forests of Central and South America, the tropic swamps of Africa. The forest growths press in, swiftly, surely, stealthily, unstayably, like a sea; the trees circle around, take root in walls and roofs, thrust boughs through window jambs, finally engulf all, until, for centuries, no one can say where they once stood, where they now stand, enjungled in warm trackless green. Then, after the lost centuries, the jungle may be searched, explored, a little cleared; and where some small settlement or village has alone been seen in the wilderness of vegetation, or not even a settlement, little by little some exquisite royal city of temples is uncovered, lying there as at the bottom of a deep, hot sargassum sea. This is what happened to the ancient Ceylon temple cities; Anuradhapura, Polonnaruwa, and other smaller groups of dagobas, many still forest-drowned.

Anuradhapura is perhaps the largest ruin anywhere; it anyhow rivals Nineveh and Babylon in size. Founded in the fifth century BC, it became the royal capital two centuries later, when it was converted to Buddhism, and received a cutting from the Sacred Bo-tree whereunder the Master had sat; the cutting grew and flowered into the sacred tree, and has flourished there for over two thousand years; if its continuity is authentic, it must be the oldest tree in the world. So Anuradhapura became a shrine for pilgrimage; magnificent monastic centre, as well as royal capital, its temples and dagobas were grouped about its green plain, and the sacred Bo-tree has seeded and given birth to a host of lesser Bo-trees. Before the precincts of the Sacred Tree is offered a mass of sweet-smelling blossoms; a monk clad in saffron yellow arranges them on an altar; the drums beat and the pipes shrill and monkeys skip about the grass. Near the Bo-tree is the collection of temple columns called the Peacock Palace, and the much larger group of the Brazen Palace – sixteen hundred columns standing together like slim tree-trunks, the only remains of the great Mahavihara built in the second century BC, which rose to many storeys, all roofed with brazen tiles, and encircled by gated walls. Inside were golden and pearl halls, an ivory throne decorated with the sun, moon and stars, and the most gorgeous furnishings in the world; it must have looked like the new Jerusalem. It was, however, not a royal palace but a monks' residence and temple. For Anuradhapura was one of the most religious cities that have ever been. The Brazen Temple has been thrown down and rebuilt, the last time in the twelfth century: the Bo-tree has, they say, never been destroyed. The four great dagobas of Anuradhapura stand about it, solid domes, inverted bowls, some still grown with scrub, some containing relics, some merely commemorative; there are a crowd of smaller humps scattered over the green landscape, like a field of toadstools, and, no doubt, many more in the jungle, as yet undiscovered. For jungle stretches all round and about Anuradhapura, and in it are doubtless more temples, more forests of grey stone pillars, more humped dagobas, which camouflage themselves as tree-grown hillocks; possibly, too, the undiscovered walls of the city, and the royal palace and secular residential town. For Anuradhapura was a great city from the fifth century BC to the ninth AD when the turbulent Tamils invaded and caused it to be abandoned. What has chiefly so far been reclaimed from the jungle is the monastic settlement. Those great assemblages of pillars, the storeyed Mahavihara, the humped dagobas, are not excessively beautiful in themselves, in spite of carved balustrades, carved moon-shaped stone slabs, sculptured Buddhas and elephants; what gives them aesthetic charm is their situation, jungle-surrounded, barely reclaimed, the green sward on which they stand, the scattered lakes, the delicious stone baths, the clammy, swooning climate which lies like warm, scented flowers on forest and clearing, the frisking monkeys, and, above all, the long reaches of the mysterious, exotic past, winding like a dimly seen river through green enjungled silence to the gorgeous heyday of royal and priestly magnificence of two thousand years ago, and beyond that to the earliest beginnings, when the Bo-tree took root. Long reaches of silence and desertion, of the slow green drowning of the insatiable jungle; following the thousand years of elegant, cruel, religious kingship, when the love of Gautama was preached and those who incurred royal displeasure were torn to pieces by elephants.

After the desertion of Anuradhapura, Polonnaruwa took its place as royal capital. It was abandoned at the end of the thirteenth century; more utterly abandoned, for not even a village marked its site; its ruins lay, and vast numbers of them still lie, unseen in the forest which engulfed them. Pushing through the eighty miles or so of jungle from Anuradhapura along the forest tracks (avoiding the road), is to journey through exotic beauty, strangely set with the half-buried ruins of an ecclesiastical Buddhist world — temples and dagobas that sprout with trees, statues and carved sculptures partly seen among the rank undergrowth, groups of monastery buildings in all stages of ruin and clearance, hermitages enclosed in great tangles of twisting tree roots, hung with brilliant flowers and skipped about by monkeys, rock baths and cisterns and large pools bright with kingfishers and full of tortoises, stone portals carved with Buddhas, elephants and cobras, groups of richly capitaled pillars, moonstone stair slabs carved with prancing animals, great monasteries of temples and pillars such as Jetawanarama, built two thousand years ago and scattered for miles through the forest, the remains of palaces, rocky hills covered with terraces and steps, grass and scrub, and finally Polonnaruwa on its lake, with the great pleasure garden the Park of Heaven, laid out by King Parakrama in the twelfth century. This must have been a glorious landscape park, set with lotus-grown pools, a dazzling and exquisite bathing hall with sandalwood pillars, a summer pavilion, a royal palace of great loveliness. All this is described in the Mahavamsa in enthusiastic and beautiful detail; we can see the ruins of each thing described, and

imagination rears the palace and park as they were. One of the loveliest things to be seen is the lotus bath — five granite flower-shaped circular steps, lying one within another, until they enclose the rose-shaped bath itself. Such carved decoration as there is (the colossal Buddhas, the charming elephants, the naïve stone dwarfs that guard the sacred places, the animals and flowers) has an engaging Cingalese grace, in keeping with the swinging bells and the scented flowers. You will not encounter in Ceylon those barbaric winged bulls and lions and bearded ox-eyed men of Assyria; the sculptured youths have long painted almond eyes and delicate hands. These de-forested ruins of ancient Buddhism lack the finest architecture and art, but they have much compensating charm. . . .

Sail across the Gulf of Siam to Indo-China: here, in Cambodia, Cochin China, Tonkin, Laos, Annam, you will find the great jungles and the hidden cities. They are possibly the most romantic in the world; none of the jungle temples or cities of Central America is as splendid as Angkor Vat and Angkor Thom; no piece of country more set with hidden beauties than the great green sea of forest that rolls over Cambodia and about the great river of Mekong. One may feel Angkor Vat too ornate, too crowded with decoration and sculpture, lacking the grand simplicity of Greece and the exquisite clustered-fruit curves of Byzantium; it may oppress with its many-coned prodigiousness, its seemingly endless stairways, corridors, towers, colonnades and fuss, its unpausing friezes of animals and men marching and capering in bas-relief, its lack of uncovered spaces, its redundancy of great bland faces of the god which have smiled so tranquilly and ironically down on all this animation for over a thousand years. One may feel this too muchness, or one may not: but, rising like a great galleon from the rolling sea, Angkor's splendour seems to belong to dreams. Indeed it has been part of men's dreams down the ages; the greatest city of that extraordinary race, the Khmers, capital of the Fu-Nan empire, holding subject a hundred and twenty kings, founded in the ninth century but destroyed and rebuilt in the twelfth, in the valley of Siem Reap, the magnificent heart of a kingdom glorious for four or five centuries; for magnificence there was nothing in the east to touch it. The golden city of lotus-crowned towers, described by Kublai Khan's ambassador, full of tombs, treasure, concubines, dancing girls, processions and religious shrines, monumental phalluses which were also religious, caparisoned elephants, palanquins, gods and slaves. The vast temple (or was it a funerary shrine of kings?) Angkor Vat, the many more whose wrecked piles stand about and around the city, all belong to those three centuries from the ninth to the twelfth; precise chronology is, archaeologists admit, guesswork, and they all contradict one another. There are Hindu influences; there is Buddha and Brahmanism; and Angkor Vat suggests the great Java ziggurat of Borobudur; but the work is the characteristic work of the Khmers at the zenith of their creative pride, since fallen into such decadent and incurious simplicity. The great era declined; there was trouble with the barbarous invading Siamese; about the year 1400 they attacked and took Angkor and the other cities; the Khmers abandoned the cities and went under, and so, it seems, did the cities, drowning slowly in the jungle that flowed over them. Both Khmers and cities have been under ever since, forest-drowned. From time to time European travellers have seen strange visions of huge carved towers, cone-shaped, scarcely rising above the rippled green, submerged ships over which the swaying seas parted and closed. In the nineteenth century Angkor was discovered and explored. A French traveller saw it in 1850; the naturalist Henri Mouhot in 1861; ruins grander, he exclaimed in delighted amaze, than any Greece or Rome had left. The Cambodians regarded it with awed mistrust; it was the work of giants, they said, or of the King of the Angels, or of the Leper King; or it made itself; they know many legends, but, it seems, little history; in this they resemble many other commentators on Angkor. When Mouhot came it was deep in jungle; it has since been cleared but not stripped bare; it still has the air, or anyhow Angkor Thom has the air, of a great ship riding a swaying, surfing sea. Angkor Vat stands in a green clearing; deeper in the jungle lies the great city, once, it was said, larger than Augustan Rome, standing on a great trade route, passing commerce through its hands like ropes of gold, now for five centuries desolate, given over to its ancient gods, to the forest, and to a dark whisper of crowding bats.

No ruin has better illustrated the great cleavage between the two divergent schools of ruin-pleasurists, the romantic and the archaeological. Since the discovery of Angkor, many volumes and many articles have appeared, most of them conceived in poetic excitement and achieving romantic inexactitude. Almost everyone who has seen these prestigious prodigies becomes temporarily an intoxicated poet. The Chinese ambassador with his golden city and the great burnished lotus flower that blazed like a beacon on the highest tower of Bayon; the French naturalist who rhapsodized over the startling vision five centuries later; Pierre Loti, who described it with a felicitous beauty even greater than his normal lushness; nearly all the twentieth-century travellers, who fall suddenly into enchantment, intoxicated by the delirious maze that piles its complications to the sky, by the stone city and its palaces and temples foundered in the engulfing forest. Pierre Loti saw a picture of it as a child; great strange towers entwined with exotic branches, and knew that he would one day see them. When he did so, in middle age, the colossal temple seemed, in the hot glare of noon, like a mirage. It took a little time before he was caught in its spell, wandering enchanted and bemused through the maze of courts, terraces, corridors, twisting stairways, between walls carved with long processions of dancing Apsaras, lovely in their smiling grace, and battling chariots and elephants, and always the musing god, cross-legged and calm. To enter the great temple by causeway and lilied moat was to be caught into some delirious dream; by night a dream of darkness, wandering through endless galleries, climbing spiralling stairs grown with grass and slippery with centuries of feet, past great towered and arcaded terraces, tree-grown, one terrace above another till from the summit he looked down on the roof of forest that waved over Angkor Thom. By night the halls were windy with the swirling, squeaking multitude of bats that hung from the roof all day, spreading their musky smell, flapping and twittering about intruders' heads. In daylight the temple is also a fantastic dream, its splendours illustrated with a more than earthly light that gleams on the sculptured dancers, the warriors, the elephants, and the gods who occupy. Pierre Loti was caught in the strangeness, the melancholy, of the sanctuary of his childish dreams, the mystery of the enigmatic race who had built their empire in these forests, flourished there for a few centuries, and departed, leaving behind their gods to hold it. Looking down from the high terrace of the temple, he surveyed the jungle which hid Angkor Thom. If we could now, he mused, cut down those branches, we should see long paved avenues, bordered by gods, seven-headed serpents, bell towers, all foundered now.

Darkness fell. The gods around him began to cause him uneasiness. A nameless horror issued from the dark recesses, trailing along the gallery; above him little rat-like cries chirped from stone ceilings. Mystery and fear enveloped him.

The Khmers too were a dark mystery; it has been the fashion to write of them as if they had no known origins and had departed into nowhere, like gods. This annoys more informed historians of Angkor, such as M. Coedès . . . who has published learned articles on Cambodian inscriptions. '*Mais peut-être*', he observes with acerbity of one such writer, '*notre écrivain a-t-il simplement cédé au goût romantique du mystère des ruines.'* He quotes with irony from Pierre Loti's *Pèlerin d'Angkor*. 'See', said Loti, 'where palaces stood, see where lived kings stupendously magnificent – of whom one knows nothing more, who passed into oblivion without leaving even one name graven on a stone or in a memory. . . .' These, adds M. Coedès, are the amateurs of mystery who sometimes reproach us for despoiling the ruins of the vegetation which hides them, and making them accessible and comprehensible.

Alas! Are we then obliged to choose between the forest which devours ruins and the conserving of the relics of the past, though it may not be impossible to reconcile the two; the example of Ta Prohm proves it, where the admirable frame of verdure and the tentacules of the cotton trees do not prevent people from visiting the monument, nor from knowing that it is a temple built in 1189 by King Jayavarman VII to the memory of his mother.

The exasperated scholar has more to say about the vague romanticism which ignores facts and heeds only the poetry of ruin and jungle. But the romantics, intoxicated with beauty, will go their way. Angkor Thom is even more to their taste than Angkor Vat – 'the winding-sheet of a town, where every stone bears traces of an antique sculpture'. Nothing in Angkor Thom is so elaborately magnificent as Angkor Vat; but the ruin is much greater; nearly all is shattered and jungle-grown, though the French have, since 1907, done some clearance and mapping of the city's plan. Cleared or uncleared, it is an extraordinary and stupendous sight. The great metropolis covered, with its palaces and temples and outlying buildings, many miles. Within the city walls a maze of wrecked beauty lies – temples, palaces, squares. Bayon, the huge step-pyramid temple, a mountainous mass of shattered terraces and high towers, god-adorned, is an architectural mystery. It has had the romantics in trembling raptures, and has baffled even the archaeologists. Parmentier, the doyen of Indo-China archaeologists, admits that, before the forest had been cleared from it, Bayon was an incomprehensible maze, but of a poignant romanticism. Loti's lyrical description sprouts with huge destructive fig-trees, strangling roots, the forest waving its greenery from every crevice and gallery, quite impossible to see what was what. Recent work has despoiled Bayon of its green shroud and of much of its romantic aspect; there emerges, clear and bare, what has been called the greatest monument of Cambodia; but they have not learnt so much about it even yet; archaeologists, bemused by this mysterious splendour, talk mistily about the bizarre pile; they gaze on it by moonlight

and refer to the Nagas, as if they were awed Khmer peasants. Round it lie strewn on the ground many more towers, and from each smiles the god, about whose identity much discussion has been held, much ink expended. Brahma, Buddha, Siva, Locesvara; anyone may think what he likes. The date, too; latest opinion seems to favour the twelfth century, not earlier. But, confounding speculations, the intricate marvel climbs to heaven, with its galleries, terraces, deep courts, steep stairways, and the high central tower that, once gold-painted, held aloft, said the Chinese ambassador, the burnished lotus, shining like a beacon over the magnificent city; and on the front terrace stood two golden lions. All is now desolate, fantastic, and ambushed with ghosts; the erroneous opinions of archaeologists twitter among them like bats. From the third terrace can be surveyed the mass of shattered walls and towers and courts that were Angkor Thom's palaces, temples, baths, colonnades. There is a great central plaza, but no theatre; the Khmers, like the Ceylonese and the Maya, were untouched by Greece and Rome; and there are no remains of ordinary houses, for these were built of earth and wood and have gone to earth and wood again, leaving no trace. Palaces, temples, monasteries, shrines, tombs: these tiled, colonnaded and sculptured buildings make the huge wilderness of ruins that spreads for miles through the dense jungle. . . .

In time, no doubt, everything will be given a name. Meanwhile, though many learned and detailed descriptions of the city and its entouraging forest suburbs appear, experts still differ: beyond their differences Angkor and its offspring incredibly sprawl through miles of jungle, some of the most prodigious, exciting, intricately wrought and sensuously moving ruins in the world. . . .

Go on from Angkor through the great forests of Indo-China and the Malay Peninsula where the paddy fields have not yet pushed them back; jungle-buried Khmer cities and temples strew the way. According to travellers one comes on them like truffles in a wood, seductively decaying in green boskage, to be dug up and plucked by any white explorers who happen along. Travellers camp by suspected mounds, pitch camp among the lunatic fringe of monkeys, mosquitoes, tigers and modern Khmers . . . and proceed to dig up ancient colonies mentioned by Ptolemy, ancient trading marts at the mouths of rivers silted up centuries ago. They find eighth-century stone images of Indian gods grown about by the trunks of huge trees; they discover in a remote valley the site of an Indian city built centuries before Angkor. . . . They seek a city; and, since there are so many cities, or fragments of cities, about, the odds are they find one, or perhaps several.

But they have not invariably been sure what it is; it may be an outlying fragment, a suburb, in the green belt of some city already known; can it, they uneasily wonder, have been after all only a part of Pra Khan, or Sambor, or Pnom Dek, or some other of the found cities? Can it even be, the newcomer to the business may fear, one of these cities themselves? Is it really a discovery? Was the city really lost, or is it only perhaps the traveller? These are riddles, and many of them must still remain so. But should his city not, after all, prove a find, the explorer need not feel discouraged, for where that came from there are plenty more; it seems that one cannot come to the end of the lost cities of the jungles, in their various stages of dilapidation and decay. Were the Khmers of today as intelligent as their forbears, they would go in for the ruin-faking business in the remote fastnesses of their forests, and then lead their white visitors, who enjoy such things, to see their handiwork. Possibly they do.

Be this as it may, the excitement and rapture of coming on these delightful objects, so solitary, so richly carved, so religious, so ruinous, so like Angkor, so very Khmer (yet sometimes with strange alien touches, such as the little Doric-looking temple at Sambor) – the excitement of tracking down and looking upon one of these forest dreams is worth all the anguish of the quest, wherein the ruin-seekers have persevered in peril of tigers, peril of snakes, peril of mosquitoes, of crocodiles, fever, thirst, exhaustion, rival explorers, and the nightmare of the tropical green dusk. . . .

The ruined temples and pagodas of Burma are not comparable with these jungle felicities. They are more elaborate, ambitious, rich in ornament, fussier, more splendid individually; they do not sprawl in great groups about dense forest; they are tabulated and known. The great ruins of Pagan have given, through the past six centuries, much pleasure, and more particularly their general view as seen from the Irrawaddy. Pagan had in its prime about thirteen thousand pagodas and monasteries; the effect of the crowd of bell-shaped, dome-shaped, pumpkin-shaped, or cross-shaped sacred buildings, standing above the great river, every variety of Buddha decorating their niches and their tiles, must have been very brilliant and glittering. Pagan, wrecked by Kublai Khan's army in anger, is still in its diminished ruins a place of shrines and pilgrimage. Since the Burmese are probably the most religious people in the world, their ruins are all sacred, even the palaces, and Buddha presides everywhere. There is a bland, smiling tranquillity about these temples and monasteries even in ruin; the Buddhas sit in their shrines unperturbed; the haunting gods are amiable, charming, even a little smug; there is no Gothic darkness, creeping ivy, bats, foxes, or melancholy owls to induce *Ruinenschmerz*, and the most shattered pagoda is still elegant and well-mannered, and not really morbid.

Angkor, Cambodia. Apsaras from the Terrace of the Leper King

157 Angkor, Cambodia. The Bayon
From tier after tier of rising stone the inscrutable faces of many Buddhas stare out from the many-towered Bayon. The vast and silent ruins of Angkor have stirred the imagination of mankind ever since an awed explorer first stumbled upon them in 1850. But it is only lately that a clear picture of the Khmer civilization has begun to emerge. The 'lost city' of Angkor is in fact an enormous complex of terraces, towers, galleries and reservoirs, the centre of a once strongly centralized empire which depended for its prosperity on the cultivation of rice and lay under the absolute control of a god-king. By means of elaborate irrigation systems two or even three crops a year could be harvested. Each reservoir had its temple, Angkor itself being only the grandest, the crown and capital of the whole kingdom.
Of the chief buildings, Angkor Vat was built by King Suryavarman II (1112–52) and Angkor Thom by Jayavarman VII (1181–1218). The Bayon lies at the centre of Angkor Thom and was among the last buildings to be completed. It is square in plan, rising through successive terraces to a high central tower. The entire surface is a mass of reliefs, so that it has been called 'really not so much a work of architecture as of sculpture'.

158 Anuradhapura, Sri Lanka. The Bo-tree
To the Buddhist pilgrim the Bo-tree, shown here rising behind the steps of the terrace on which it stands, is the most sacred object in Anuradhapura. It is said to be a cutting from the tree under which Buddha was sitting when he received Enlightenment. Tradition relates that when King Asoka in the third century BC sent his son and daughter to bring Buddhism to Sri Lanka, they took with them a branch from the parent tree (which had spontaneously planted itself in a golden vase for the journey). The cutting was installed at Anuradhapura and has flourished there ever since, 'always green, never growing, never decaying'. If this is true (and the fact that it has been continuously watched over by a succession of guardians makes it perfectly plausible), it must be the oldest historical tree in the world. The city was the capital of Sri Lanka and a centre of Buddhist pilgrimage from the third century BC to the eighth century AD.

159 Sigiriya, Sri Lanka. An Apsaras
The nymphs of Hindu mythology are portrayed with richly sensuous charm in the sixth-century AD frescoes at Sigiriya ('Lion Rock'), the fortress-palace of King Kassapa. The place was hollowed out of the living rock.

160–1 Polonnaruwa, Sri Lanka. Gal Vihara
Buddha lies in death, one arm along his body, the other under his head, an attitude of sublime serenity. For Buddha's death was the attainment of *nirvana*—the final transcendence of the self, escape from the cycle of existence. The smaller standing statue may also be Buddha. But many experts think it could be his cousin and favourite disciple Ananda.

162 Polonnaruwa, Sri Lanka. The lotus bath
'. . . a gigantic lotus flower of granite, full blown, 24 feet 9 inches in diameter, with five concentric lamina of eight petals, gradually diminishing to a stamen'—even the sober language of the Sri Lanka Archaeological Survey Report blossoms into poetry when it describes this charming fantasy of the builder's art.

163 Polonnaruwa, Sri Lanka. Gal Vihara
The lotus flowers on the soles of the Buddha's feet are one of the key symbols of Buddhism. With its roots in the slime of the earth and its pure blossoms reaching up to the sunlight, it stands for the dual nature of man.

164 Anuradhapura, Sri Lanka. The Northern Dagoba
These great dagobas—circular domed shrines erected over relics of Buddha or one of his disciples, and surrounded by an ambulatory for the pilgrims—dominate Anuradhapura. Some have been cleared and restored. Others, like the Northern Dagoba (fourth century AD), are still so covered with vegetation that they look like hills rising above the forest.

165 Amarapura, Burma. Seated Buddha
In this image from the precincts of the Patadawgyi Pagoda the Buddha is portrayed in the gesture of taking the Earth to witness, representing the Buddha's victory over Mara.

166 Angkor, Cambodia. An Apsaras from Angkor Vat
Nude to the waist, slender and sensuous, these dancing nymphs, carved with exquisite art, appear all over the temples of Angkor. They wear skirts of rich material shown blowing back in conventional perspective. The flowered background, the subtle rhythm of their gestures, the fantastic luxury of their jewelled necklaces and diadems bring to exotic life the paradise after death promised to the subjects of the Khmer Empire by their divine overlords.

167 Angkor, Cambodia. The god Vishnu, from a frieze at Angkor Vat
Vishnu rides in his chariot amid worshippers. Of the Hindu Trinity (Brahma, Vishnu and Siva), he is the most benevolent.

168 Angkor, Cambodia. Sculpture at Ta Prohm
Giant trees have forced their way through the stones. Silent shattered figures of gods lie festooned beneath the creeping shadows of the jungle. Ta Prohm is one of the smaller temple-compounds of Angkor.

169 Angkor, Cambodia. Ta Prohm
High-crowned and smiling, Apsaras watch over the entrance of Ta Prohm. The temple, whose sculpture is in the same style as that of the Bayon, was erected in 1186 by Jayavarman VII in memory of his mother.

170–1 Amarapura, Burma. Precincts of the Patadawgyi Pagoda
A mythical beast from China, the meditating figure of an

Indian Buddha and, in the distance, a pagoda, unique product of the merging of cultures—these sum up the varied forces that have gone to the making of Burma. The ruined site is Amarapura—'the immortal city', but its history belies its title. Founded in 1783 it lasted as the capital of Burma (with an interval from 1822 to 1837) only until 1859.

172 *Pagan, Burma. Tomb and pagoda*
'It might pass for a scene in another planet,' wrote an English traveller, Captain Yule, in 1855, 'so fantastic and unearthly was the architecture.' In the thirteenth century, before Kubla Khan destroyed it, Pagan must indeed have been a fairy-tale city. It extended for some twenty miles along the bank of the Irrawaddy river and contained at least 13,000 pagodas!

173 *Pagan, Burma. The Bupaya Pagoda*
'. . . like a great pumpkin with the thick end uppermost, a simple spire rising from the top and a succession of concentric sloping walls and parapets crowned with trefoils'. So Captain Yule described the Bupaya, or Pumpkin Pagoda. It was built by one of the early kings of Pagan,

probably in the ninth century A D. The little shrine in the foreground was added later.

174–5 *Pagan, Burma. Passages in the That-byinnu Pagoda*
This, the highest pagoda in Pagan, was built about 1144 and has a square plan. Its big vestibule opens on to stairs leading up to a higher level where there is a corridor all round the interior. The core of the building is solid brick. Deep in the centre, approached through many doors and inner chambers, stands the image of Buddha 'That-byinnu' (the All-Knowing).

176 *Pagan, Burma. A pagoda*
The remains of over 5000 pagodas are still visible at Pagan—domed, bell-shaped, pyramidal, square, octagonal or circular—all originally topped by gilded cupolas or spires.

177 *Polonnaruwa, Sri Lanka. The Palace*
The royal Palace of Polonnaruwa, made of brick, and raised on a square stone platform, was ornamented with pilasters. It dates from the end of the thirteenth century, the reign of King Wijayo Bahn IV.

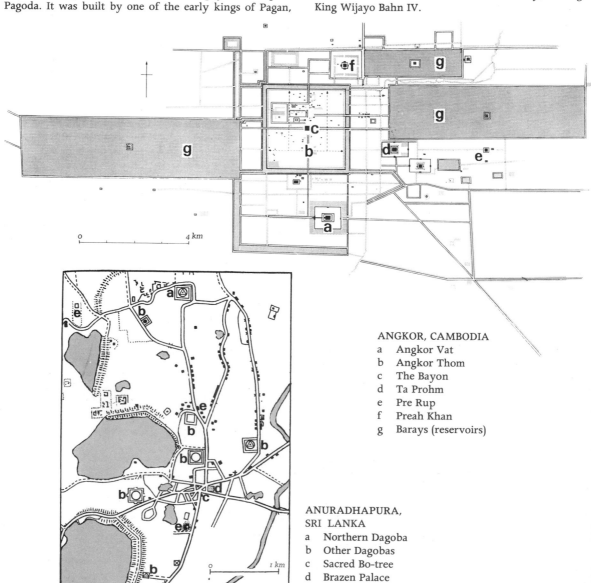

ANGKOR, CAMBODIA
a   Angkor Vat
b   Angkor Thom
c   The Bayon
d   Ta Prohm
e   Pre Rup
f   Preah Khan
g   Barays (reservoirs)

ANURADHAPURA,
SRI LANKA
a   Northern Dagoba
b   Other Dagobas
c   Sacred Bo-tree
d   Brazen Palace
e   Tombs

171

A GALAXY OF TEMPLES

Indian ruined temples need a volume to themselves; they are strewn as thickly as a galaxy. . . . All over the richly idolatrous sub-continent the ruined temples and monasteries stand. What ruins most gracefully is anyone's choice. Some prefer the decorative sculptured pillars of the eighth-century chaitya which is the most beautiful of the Ajanta cave temples; the richly worked shafts and capitals achieve an aesthetic effect more pleasing than the more primitive type of temple or monastery cell. Again, the delicate and profuse elaboration of Jain decoration takes on, in ruin, a peculiarly appealing melancholy grace. One may prefer the Indo-Aryan of the north, or the Dravidian of the south, or the pillared Buddhist stupa, or the verandahed and courted vihara. Till the Mogul conquest checked it, Indian architecture grew in grandeur and grace, and in a dozen different styles. Mountains are crowded with exquisite Jain temples in ruin; the more magnificent Dravidian vimanas stand about the south-east in almost Assyrian splendour. Out of the temples they found, the invaders built their mosques; some they adapted, purging them, sometimes more, sometimes less, of idolatrous ornament, many they destroyed and rebuilt. The mosque of Quwwat ul near Delhi boasts in an inscription of being built out of twenty-seven Jain temples. The mosques in ruin now mingle, inimically and beautifully, with their destroyed victims; Jain columns, stripped of carvings, support Moslem domes. Sometimes carvings of flowers remain. The ruined mosques have, on the whole, less beauty; they did not flower from such animated idolatrous imagination, they are less rare and fantastic. They are fewer; they do not lie in disintegrated groups over mountain and plain, delighting the eyes with intricate carved creatures.

There is a case for thinking that mosques are all the better for a touch of ruin; it imparts to the bland and confident rotundity of their domes, the regularity of their colonnaded courts, the assertiveness of their minarets, that note of pathos which their triumphant builders themselves gave to so many thousands of the temples of other faiths. . . . The carvings of living creatures, of men and gods and animals and trees which make many Hindu . . . temples so animated and enchanting, they hack away as blasphemies; the destroyers, who cannot trust themselves to look on sculptured forms or female faces without paying them improper attention, adorn their places of prayer with painted or mosaic circles, flourishes, scrolls, squares, abstract patterns, and cries of devotion and praise. . . .

Of Halebid, in Mysore, only one street is traceable in the ruined eleventh-century city, destroyed by the Mohammedan armies two centuries later. Sites can be identified, and there are two very beautiful temples; the larger and less ruined is entirely covered with carved scrolls and friezes, elephants, tigers, birds, horsemen, dancers, epics of conquest. The smaller temple, almost equally remarkable, was many years ago torn to pieces by a tree growing in its entrails. . . . At Konarak, the celebrated Black Pagoda stands magnificent in huge ruin, its great porch alone upright, a stupendous fantasy of carving (much of it erotic), tumbled horses and elephants, and piles of stone. Not far off is Bhuvaneswar, ancient capital of Orissa, now to be its capital again, the centre of an immense district of temples mostly in ruin; round the sacred lake seven thousand temples once lay; there are now a few hundred, all ruinous, representing about six centuries of Orissan art. . . .

The world is strewn with . . . missed opportunities; one marvels at the limits of the folly of our folly-minded forbears. Why, for instance, did no one set up in his grounds (I think they did not) . . . a ruined Hindu temple with erotic carvings? Classical temples abound, and mosques, and Chinese pagodas, and rotundas, nymphaeums, arches, porticoes, broken columns, castles, Gothic towers. . . .

British sightseers have . . . flocked to Elephanta Island off Bombay, to see the cave temple and its remarkable statuary. The huge stone elephant no longer stands on guard at the landing-place, for its head fell off and it was carted away to the Victoria Gardens in Bombay. But there remains the temple cut out of the rock in the eighth century, some of its pillars still standing, the Lingam shrine with its stone door-keepers, and the huge magnificent wall relief of the versatile three-faced Siva; the whole temple is so impressive and odd that it has always been a favourite excursion from Bombay; tea is served in a bungalow near the landing-place, and the Prince of Wales was given a banquet there in 1875; it was the kind of place in which royalty takes great pleasure. Bishop Heber, too. The elephant was there in his day, three times as large as life. As he climbed up the path from the landing-stage, winding prettily through woods, he was reminded of his

Hodnet rectory home. The sculptures, he complained, had suffered from the vulgar love of collecting knick-knacks and specimens which prevailed among the English more than among most nations. But the great cave, with its colonnaded portico, its temple hall, courts and shrines, its concourse of sculptured divinities, an animated *turba deorum* that gives an alarmingly populated feeling, together with several surrounding caves, smaller but also polytheous, is truly magnificent. So, indeed, are the rock temples of Ellora in Hyderabad – Buddhist, Brahmin and Jain, hewn out of the hillside with their chapels, courts, columns, shrines, galleries, statues, carvings, elephants and gods, the finest of which, the Dravidian Brahmin temple of Kailas, is one of the most beautiful things in India, and unique in kind, being a monolithic temple from which the rock has been cut away; it stands in a great court, and is richly carved within and without. Battered by a millennium of years, by the quakings of the earth, and by the furious iconoclasm of Moslems, the firm embedding of most of these cave temples in their rocky matrix has preserved them largely intact; enough damage to qualify as ruin, too little to harm them. They are, of course, comparative parvenus among Indian cave temples; the solid permanence and near invulnerability which almost disqualifies them for these pages is even more noticeable in the cave temples of the first few centuries A D and the second and third centuries B C, such as those of Ajanta and Karli and (most ancient of all) Barabar. One compares these rock-hewn sanctuaries with the temple of Buddh Gaya, probably the oldest sculptured building in India, founded in the sixth century B C, built at various times during the next four centuries, containing the sacred Bo-tree beneath which the master sat, branches from which have been planted and have flowered over the Buddhist world. The temple with its carved railings of the second century B C, a holy shrine for world pilgrimage, was restored by Burmese Buddhists in the fourteenth century, and again and more destructively by them in the nineteenth; it could scarcely have been worse done. Much of it was knocked about and broken; Sir Edwin Arnold saw hundreds of broken sculptures, some exquisitely carved with the adventures of Buddha, lying about on rubbish piles.

Buddh Gaya, India. The temples at dawn

182–3 Konarak, India. Wheels and lion from the lower platform of the Black Pagoda
Every inch of the surface, even the spokes and hub of the wheels, is covered with decoration of fantastic intricacy. The scenes along the frieze at the bottom deal mainly with the hunting of elephants. The other carvings, which have given Konarak its dubious notoriety, are highly erotic: they show couples in a variety of amorous positions, some definitely perverse. It is hard for the Western mind, nourished on Christianity, to associate these figures with a religious message, but they must be seen as part of the cult of the Sun, the source of life, and as expressing the significance of sexual union as a mystical experience. 'A man embraced by a beloved woman', says one of the *Upanishads*, 'knows nothing more of a within or without.' The whole temple of Konarak (mid-thirteenth century) was conceived as a vast replica in stone of the chariot of the sun-god Surya, but it was never finished, perhaps because the complexity of its design defeated even its ambitious builders.

184 Konarak, India. Girl musician from the Black Pagoda
Over-lifesize statues of girls playing drums and cymbals stand on the terraces of the roof, and were meant to be seen from a distance—hence their monumental proportions.

185 Konarak, India. Figure on the East Façade of the Black Pagoda
Above the main gate, on the same level as the girl musicians, stands the strange three-headed figure of Trikala Bhairava, one of the forms of Siva.

186 Buddh Gaya, India. The Mahabodi Temple
Eighty years ago this was still (in spite of some modifications by the Burmese) essentially a sixth-century temple. But in 1880 it was decided to 'restore' it with drastic thoroughness. The result was that almost every stone we now see is new. In the foreground is the sacred tree, or its descendant, in whose honour the temple stands.
It was under the Bo-tree of Buddh Gaya that Buddha, in his thirty-fifth year, received Enlightenment. King Asoka built a temple there, probably to enclose the sacred tree. It was subsequently rebuilt with great splendour. When Hiuen Tsang, a Chinese traveller, saw it in AD 635 the temple had golden statues of Buddha in its niches and another larger figure made, according to Hiuen Tsang, of 'perfumed paste'.

187 Mahabalipuram, India. The Shore Temple
A low granite ridge next to the sea in south-eastern India is the site of extraordinary excavations, carvings and monolithic temples dating from the time of the Pallava kings who ruled the Deccan in the seventh century AD. At the end of the ridge, literally on the seashore itself, are the shrines shown here. Other temples are said to have sunk beneath the sea, and at low tide glimpses of carved stones and buildings can be caught under the water.

188 Konarak, India. Detail of a statue of the god Surya from the Black Pagoda
The sun-god himself (over 8 feet tall) is portrayed in a deliberately archaic style, static and symmetrical, inviting the prayers of his worshippers.

189 Halebid, India. Detail of a dvarapala (door guardian) from the Hoysalesvara Temple
Sculptural virtuosity reached its climax in the Hoysalesvara Temple—some critics even speak of over-ripeness and decadence. But the magical delicacy of the work, its flowing lines and patterned elaboration, create an effect which, however rich, is never confused.

190 Halebid, India. The Bull Nandi from the Hoysalesvara Temple
Nandi, the sacred Bull of Siva, sits majestically at rest beneath his pavilion. The pillars supporting the roof are of superb workmanship; of the same stone as the figures on the east front, they curve so smoothly that they seem to have been turned on a lathe.

191 Halebid, India. The Bull Nandi from the Hoysalesvara Temple
Nandi is portrayed kneeling, hung with necklaces and pendant jewellery. He is 16 feet long and 10 feet high.

192 Halebid, India. Detail of the East Front of the Hoysalesvara Temple
This photograph gives some idea of the profusion of ornament that covers the temple from top to bottom. 'In the lowest tier is an endless defile of elephants, symbols of stability; next a row of lions, emblems of valour; above a tier of horsemen for speed, and in still higher horizontal registers, *makaras* and *hamsa*, the geese, or birds of Brahma.' The file of elephants is in fact 710 feet long and contains not less than 2000 animals.

193 Bhuvaneswar, India. Apsaras from the doorway of the Rajarani Temple
A dancing nymph from the Hindu paradise guards the door of the Rajarani Temple (c. AD 1000), one of the more modest of the 7000 shrines that once encircled the sacred lake of Bhuvaneswar.

194 Bhuvaneswar, India. A temple
The sikhara, a tower shaped like part of an ear of corn and marking the position of a sanctuary, is the most characteristic form in Hindu architecture.

195 Ellora, India. The Indra Sabha Temple
Entire temples cut out of rock faces were known in India from early Buddhist times (third and second centuries BC); sometimes whole monasteries with statues and halls shaped in imitation of wooden or stone buildings were hollowed out of the cliffs. At Ajanta (see Plate 197) the cliff-face is perpendicular. At Ellora it slopes more gently and in consequence the Ellora caves often have forecourts like the one shown here with entrance wall, porch and columns and

statuary left standing when the rest of the rock was excavated. The 'building' on the right is a chapel with the quadruple image of one of the twenty-four immortal Jain saints. The Jains, who carved the Indra Sabha in the mid-ninth century AD, owe their religion to Hinduism but are regarded as heretical.

196 Ellora, India. Detail from the Kailasanath Temple
The square stone pillar (*dwajastambha*), 45 feet high, is part of a temple excavated (one cannot say 'built') between AD 725 and 755. Dedicated to Siva, the temple was intended as an architectural symbol of Mount Kailasa, in the Himalayas, Siva's own eternal home. The pillar stands in the forecourt and is one of two flanking the shrine to Siva's Bull (Nandi). This rather enigmatic view is taken through an opening in the shrine's upper storey and only the middle section of the *dwajastambha* is visible. The ground plan (below) makes its position clearer.

197 Ajanta, India. Cave XXVI
Its roof carved into ribs and 'supported' by a colonnade of richly decorated columns, Cave XXVI is 68 feet long and 31 feet high. Above the columns runs a frieze showing incidents in the life of Buddha. This is only one of 29 caves at Ajanta, cut into the cliff-face between 200 BC and AD 650

198 Elephanta Island, India. The Cave Temple
Through the door—one of four, each guarded by two *dvarapalas* (door-keepers)—stands the sacred *lingam* of Siva, a cylindrical stone, 3 feet high. The temple of Elephanta was cut into a rocky island outside Bombay harbour in the sixth or seventh century AD. Six rows of columns seem to support the roof (note the brackets above the capitals) and round the sides are reliefs showing the legends of Siva.

199 Konarak, India. Temple horse from the Black Pagoda
Inevitably one compares this head with the famous horse's head from the Parthenon pediment. In spite of the gulf between the two (nearly two thousand years, plus the difference of two alien cultures and religions), something of the same delight in physical nature informs them both.

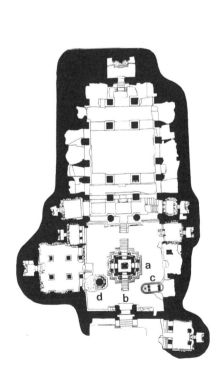

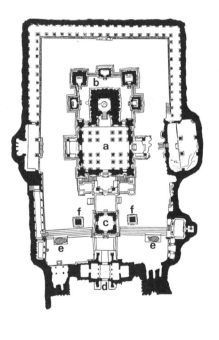

ELLORA, INDIA
Kailasanath Temple
a Porch to main shrine
b Main shrine
c Nandi shrine
d Entrance porch
e Elephants
f Dwajastambha (emblem pillars)

ELLORA, INDIA
Indra Sabha Temple
a Shrine of Jain saint
b Entrance porch
c Elephant
d Column

HALEBID, INDIA
Hoysalesvara Temple
a Nandi pavilions (north unfinished)
b East Front

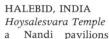

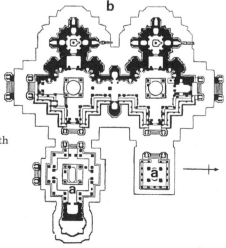

191

195

IV Pleasures and palaces

All over the world palaces stand ruined. Crumbling palaces, shattered palaces, palaces engulfed by green forests, palaces drowned in the sea, palaces whose only remnants are a few prostrate broken columns, a sprawl of foundations, grass-grown, in colours that were bright two thousand years ago. Palaces like Priam's, scarcely now to be identified among the rubbled trenches that were Ilium; palace castles like Santameri where the Frankish Dukes of Athens held their court at Thebes, of which one massive tower still stands, palaces like Sans Souci that a black king built at Haiti, palaces beneath the desert like Nineveh and Babylon, palaces beneath the sea like those of emperors round the Naples bay, palaces of the Caesars sprawled over the Palatine hill, palaces of Cyprus, where (says Dante) the Lusignan princes led a beastly life among the beastly Cypriotes, palaces huge and containing towns, like Diocletian's at Spalato, palaces at Delhi, Mistra, Tiryns, Mycenae, Persepolis, Peking, palaces rising out of lakes all about Rajputana, palaces built by Norman kings for their pleasure in Sicily, palaces covering twice five miles of fertile ground with walls and towers and domes of pleasure at Xanadu. Palaces everywhere; and more beneath the earth that we shall never see, so deeply over them have piled and silted the sands of Syria, the river mud of Sybaris, the brittle but immobile cities of the world. . . .

Antiquity is not an essential element in the romantic splendour of mouldering palaces. There is, for instance, King Christophe's huge Haitian palace of Sans Souci, built in 1812 on the precipitous mountains above the village of Milot, twenty-five miles from the sea, and now a magnificent tropical ruin, five-storeyed, rising above a balustraded terrace on the sweeping double flight of a grand stairway that suggests Versailles. The black king of Haiti determined that his palace should be finer than any in Europe, and more particularly than any in France. It was the palatial glory of the new world, piling up, terrace upon terrace, up the forested mountains above the Plaine du Nord, overlooking the distant sea. It is built of brick and stone and yellow stucco, now peeling and flaking off, and out of the walls and windows and columns and arches trees and creepers push; it is, like all tropical ruins, being drowned in engulfing vegetation.

Stupendous in size and beauty, it spreads like a walled town; its courtyards, guest-houses, stables, arsenal, barracks, domed chapel, gardens of fruit and flowers are on the scale of Knole; the sun-drenched, forest-beleaguered, golden-hued pile, with its arches, grass-grown terraces and balustrade, and the glorious sweep of stairway, stand against the forest and mountain with an indescribable effect of grandeur decadent, rich pomp fallen but still proud. Inside, all is ruin, goats and lizards and scorpions dart among the tangle of tropical orange and banana trees and heavy blossoming shrubs that grow from the broken mosaic marble floors of banquet halls and audience chambers, the polished panelling is torn from the walls, the Louis XIV gilding tarnished and smashed. Christophe had a magnificent library, paintings and tapestries and great mirrors were brought from Europe that the black emperor should outclass his white rivals. Indeed he thought of things that had not occurred to them; such as the running of a mountain stream beneath the halls to cool them; it flowed through a marble arch into a marble basin, as in Moorish and Persian palaces, so that always there was a sound of water. Christophe loved water, and his palace is also full of bathrooms. Colour, too, he loved; the blue and red and gold of his decorations, faded and mouldered, are still here and there vivid like flowers.

Looking up at the roofless jungled structure, with its long rows of windows, it is strange to imagine the negro court, with its brilliant coloured pageantry, its so dressy pomp and circumstance, its brightly decorated ebony dukes, counts and barons ceremoniously coming and going at the behest of their magnificent prince set up on his gorgeous throne for the admiration of his royal brothers in Europe and of all the West Indians of the Caribbees. . . .

In another mood . . . we climb the hill on the road to Tibur, where Hadrian's Villa lies, among olive-groves and vines, with the high line of Monte Calvo behind. Its ruins are so extensive that it used, before excavation, to be thought by the Campagna peasants the remains of a town, a predecessor of Tivoli; they called it Tivoli Vecchio. Even after centuries of excavation and archaeological research, not all is clear in the magnificent *Trümmerfeld* of this great palace town, this huge Folly of the second century, which must have given its creator such infinite pleasure to construct. For Hadrian's Villa was a work of piety, a monument to what he had always loved best in the world – the beautiful things he had seen on his travels. Travelling abroad, seeing foreign sights, restoring and improving them, taking some of them back to Rome, building temples and theatres and arches and forums, and adding whole new quarters to Greek and Eastern cities (to be called Adrianopolis) – these were his noble and generous pastimes. He had, says Audrollet, *'la manie de la pierre et du ciment'*; and he was accompanied on his travels by a legion of architects and masons, and sowed buildings all along his route. But most he liked to see things; it was his ruling passion, and what he called touring the empire was a labour of love, an enthusiastic adventure among the beauties of art and of nature (he was, among other things, an ardent mountaineer), and famous ruins, such as Ilium, Thebes and Nauplia sent him into ecstasies. He returned from his first empire tour in A D 125, and settled at Tivoli, where, upon a villa already in existence, he started the planning and building of his great rambling inconsequent palace. Yet, though it rather wears that air, inconsequent it was not; he had a definite scheme and plan for it; it was to reproduce the buildings, even the landscapes, that had given him so much pleasure in Greece and Egypt. He gave them the names of their prototypes abroad – the Lyceum, the Academy, the Prytaneum, the Pœcile, the Canopus, the Vale of Tempe, with the Peneus flowing through; and by these names they are, rightly or wrongly, identified today. . . .

Entering by a cypress avenue from the Tivoli road, one passes on one side a Greek theatre, on the other, in the distance, the Vale of Tempe and the Peneus; overlooking the Vale is a fine groved terrace. The path leads on to . . . the imitation of the Canopus, that celebrated and popular Alexandrian pleasure canal bordered by hostelries and booths leading to the temple of Serapis. How far Hadrian's canal, bordered by amusement booths, and ending in the large vaulted temple surrounded with fountains and decorated with frescoes and statues, resembled its original, it is hard to say; but making it and using it for parties of pleasure on pretended trips to Serapis must have been the greatest fun, even if the orgies en route fell short of Alexandrian form. . . .

By the time one has walked the several miles of this palatial ramble, one has a great affection for its charming, eager, erudite, art-loving, pleasure-loving and immensely vain creator, who so expended his imagination and wealth in building images of the beauty he had seen, who collected the rich store of statues (many were of the drowned and beloved Antinous as a god) which were found and removed from the palace during the centuries of excavation; who entertained his friends on such a lordly scale, who built lecture halls, exquisitely decorated banqueting rooms, libraries, theatres, swimming baths, pleasure canals, who sought to bring Greece and Egypt, Elysium and the infernal regions to his Tivoli hillside, constructing this great marble town of assorted and beautiful buildings and gardens, this stupendous and learned Folly.

The villa was added to after Hadrian's death, down to the time of Diocletian. It must have been largely destroyed by Totila when he sacked Tivoli; what was left of it stood decaying through the Middle Ages, and was pillaged for its sculptures and mosaics during the Renaissance, in the usual destructive manner, regardless of damage to structure. 'Unfortunately for it,' wrote Gaston Boissier, 'Hadrian's villa turned out to be much richer in such things than all the other ruins that had been excavated. It became for three centuries a kind of inexhaustible mine which furnished masterpieces to all the museums in the world. . . .' Indeed, even more pleasure has been derived from the villa in ruin than during the centuries of its glorious heyday. . . .

The romanticism of Chateaubriand was . . . richly fed by this immense ruin-maze, grown over with wild verdure that charmed the eye and saddened the heart: 'never were heaven and earth, the works of nature and of man, better mingled in a picture.' Wandering over the ruins, he felt himself transported to Greece and Egypt, Elysium and Hades. He was, in fact, the visitor for whom the villa was designed. He did not leave it without filling his pockets with small pieces of porphyry, alabaster, verd-antique and mosaic, and noting how other people had written their names on the marble walls, hoping to prolong their existence by attaching to celebrated places a souvenir of their existence; but, he decided, they deceived themselves.

Before the ruins were stripped of their shrubs and flowers in the 1870s, they must have been fantastically beautiful. . . . Later, the destroying hand of the ruin-clearers got to work, and in 1875 Augustus Hare complained that, with the flowers rooted up, the ruins stripped of their creepers and of their fringe of lovely shrubs, the Villa Adriana was little worth a visit. He was of that school of romantics which likes its ruins picturesquely served up. But those who do not today find the villa beautiful, exciting and grand, sprawling over its olive and cypress slopes and valleys, the shattered, fantastic palace of a cultivated, pleasure-loving and whimsical emperor and patron of the arts, had better spend their Tivoli visit, as Evelyn did, in the ingenious gardens of the Villa d'Este, or looking at the cascades and the temples and guessing at the site of Horace's villa. . . .

More substantial is the palace that Diocletian built at Spalato, and where he spent his last nine years living in luxurious retirement and growing cabbages.

'Reason dictated, and content seems to have accompanied, his retreat,' as Gibbon observed. No one who has seen this magnificent palace can be surprised. It has always, both before and after it took on (in the seventh century) its present eccentric and unique appearance of a town enclosed in a palace, produced a stupendous effect on those who have visited it. . . .

Diocletian's is one of the few Roman imperial villas now standing moderately intact; it is also the largest. . . . It has been, possibly, the most serviceable ruin in the world, for it contains several hundred houses and several thousand inhabitants, besides a whole medieval town of narrow streets and small squares, clustering about the few Roman buildings that remain. The refugees from the ruined Salona, after fleeing from the detestable Avars to the islands, crept back to shelter themselves behind the walls of the great abandoned palace, blocking up the arched windows of the long cryptoporticus that ran the length of the wall above the sea, destroying halls and courts and colonnades so as to fit in their little dwellings and streets, turning a Roman palace into a medieval slum, turning pagan temples and a mausoleum into Christian churches. With its backing of mountains and its long arcaded façade rising from the sea, and the wide bay of ships before it stretching east and west between sheltering juts of land, the square palace town lying amid its outer fortifications and the sprawl of modern town that has grown up outside its walls, astonishes the eye and mind. 'As we skirt its waterfront for about six hundred feet we gradually understand that there is no parallel to what we are seeing,' a professor of archaeology from the new world wrote forty years ago; 'a medieval city of nearly twenty thousand people built largely inside the walls of an imperial fortified villa-palace, planned like a military camp and yet a monument of luxury and magnificence.' Visitors to Spalato have always said much the same of it, since the Emperor Constantine Porphyrogenitus commented in the tenth century that it surpassed, even in its ruin, all powers of description. It was admired and described by sixteenth-, seventeenth- and eighteenth-century travellers; but the first accurate and detailed survey, that publicised it in Europe, was Robert Adam's monumental work of description and engraving. Adam, who had a great desire to 'add the observation of a private residence of the Ancients to my study of their public works', and who, apparently, had not visited the recently discovered Pompeii or Herculaneum, travelled to Dalmatia in 1754 to inspect the palace of which he had heard so much, taking with him the French artist, Clérisseau, and two draughtsmen. What he wanted to see was one of the magnificent villas described by the Romans, such as Pliny's, with the additional grandeur given it by that noble and extravagant imperial architect whose structures he had admired in Rome and elsewhere. . . .

Medieval towers and walls, Venetian fortifications, destroyed arcades and colonnades, Christianized temples, had made a confusion of the palatial scheme which needed great skill to sort out. But Adam's views and plans have admirable lucidity as well as beauty, and have been the chief guide to the palace ever since. Even the French archaeologist, Cassas, full of patriotic jealousy forty years later, who complained that Adam had seen everything with the cold egotism of his nation, plagiarized from him freely and without acknowledgment. Since Adam, there has been restoration, renovation and reconstruction, not all good: but in the main the palace-town is as he saw and drew it. There is the long arcaded cryptoporticus on the sea wall, its arches filled in with green-shuttered dwellings and shops; here the emperor took his walks, and from the chamber at the western end saw the sunset like a rose beyond the bay; of the fifty Doric columns between the arches, forty remain; of the four gates there are three.

Entering by the Porta Aurea in the north wall, an arched portal beneath a row of arcaded niches where statues once stood (something in the style of Theodoric's palace at Ravenna) one walks between medieval houses and shops to where the residential part of the palace and the Roman buildings begin. Before us is the arcaded peristylium, now the Piazza del Duomo, its arcades filled up with medieval and later houses and buildings; it is rich in sculptured decoration; its Corinthian pillars, mostly intact, are of rose granite and cipollino; the doors and balconies between them do not spoil the effect. Adam's engraving shows merchants selling bales of cloth, and women washing clothes, beneath the rich friezes and capitals, and marble lattices with shrubs pushing up through the pavement, and a sphinx couchant beside the steps leading into the portico of the vestibule. A colossal modern bronze statue of a bishop by Mestrovik stands incongruously there today. A great quadrangular atrium opens on to the cryptoporticus, that tremendous gallery above the sea wall once decorated all along its length with statues and sculpture and paintings. Off the gallery is a row of large rooms; all the usual accommodation of a large Roman villa, but on the immense and majestic scale suited to an emperor. It is less ambitious and romantically exciting than Hadrian's villa; Diocletian, a century and a half later, had not that picturesque and world-embracing artistic taste; and architecture and sculpture had both begun to decline. But it is a better specimen of an imperial villa; to study its scheme and plan is to realize more precisely the Roman way of life. And it has the eternally attractive romance of the accretions of the ages; medieval built on to classical, pagan turning Christian; it is one of the best examples in the world of picturesque life in a ruin. Diocletian's octagonal domed mausoleum became a Christian church when the refugees from Salona settled there, then a cathedral, its original beauty and decoration visible under its fourteenth- and fifteenth-century interior work and the recent unfortunate restorations. In spite of these, it is the only imperial tomb preserved almost intact. Outside, it is more beautiful, the medieval campanile erected in what was its portico is, though incongruous and much restored, attractive. To the west of it, almost entire, the heavily friezed and portalled baptistery, once a temple, with its waggon roof and rich carvings, is a beautiful example of its period and style. It is surrounded by charming sculptured fragments, and by a jumble of houses.

To walk about the nine acres or so of city between the palace walls is delightful. Everywhere about the narrow medieval streets are Venetian houses and palaces, balconies and windows, among modern shops and cafés, Roman colonnades, pretty courtyards, and stairs, fragments of ancient friezes and bas-reliefs on houses and gates; the medley recalls, as it should, the late empire with an Oriental touch, the Dalmatian Middle Ages, the Venetian and Hungarian régimes. Much of the imperial stone, pulled down by the settlers, is still to be seen in the medieval houses.

The town outside the palace walls sprawls westward between mountains and sea, Venetian towers and palace and a labyrinth of narrow streets round the great Piazza dei Signori and the smaller Piazza del Mercato down by the quay. Split is now a thriving capital city, full of hotels, modern shops, casinos, cafés, bathing beach, and all a capital should have. But, so long as its great palace stands there, holding the medieval town close within its arcaded walls, it will remain the *palatium*, the last great imperial palace, Diocletian's seaside villa outside his noble Roman city of Salona, the capital of Dalmatia. . . .

Ruin and royalty make the best juxtaposition. . . . It is the contrast of the high past splendour with present dilapidation that dramatizes the rich and noble decay of the deserted palaces, Hindu and Mogul, of India. Of these, perhaps the most lovely is the marble palace in the deserted Hindu city of Amber in Rajputana. There are several palaces in Amber . . . the finest is the great ivory-hued marble early seventeenth-century building, standing on a jut of hill above the lake (which

once mirrored it, but is now almost dry), an unearthly palace shining in creamy magnolia pallor, with latticed galleries, gilded balconies, alabaster mosaics and sculptures, pillared Hall of Audience, fountained garden jewelled with smaller palaces and temples, the whole climbing in terraces above the lake, gate beyond gate, court beyond court. Inside, suites of exquisite, inlaid, haunted rooms; 'scores of venomous and suggestive little rooms', where was lived 'the riotous, sumptuous, murderous life' to which the British government, said Kipling sixty years ago, has put an end. His description of the palace is worth quoting:

'He passed under iron-studded gates whose hinges were eaten out with rust, and by walls plumed and crowned with grass, and under more gateways, till at last he reached the palace, and came suddenly into a great quadrangle where two blinded, arrogant stallions, covered with red and gold trappings, screamed and neighed at each other from opposite ends of the vast space. . . . If, as Viollet-le-Duc tells us to believe, a building reflects the character of its inhabitants, it must be impossible for one reared in an Eastern palace to think straightly or speak freely. . . . The cramped and darkened rooms, the narrow smooth-walled passages with recesses where a man might wait for his enemy unseen, the maze of ascending and descending stairs leading nowhither, the ever-present screens of marble tracery . . . all these things breathe of plot and counter-plot, league and intrigue. . . . The Englishman wandered into all parts of the palace, for there was no one to stop him – not even the ghosts of the dead Queens – through ivory-studded doors into the women's quarters. . . . A creeper had set its hands upon the lattice there, and there was the dust of old nests in one of the niches in the walls. . . . There were questions innumerable to be asked in each court and keep and cell; but the only answer was the cooing of the pigeons.'

Thirty years before Kipling, Louis Rousselet was given leave by the Rajah to stay in the palace while he explored Amber; he and his companions spent five weeks there; it could not, he felt, have been nicer. He chose for his residence the charming Jess Munder pavilion, all delicate marble trellis work and sparkling mosaics, and a handsome terrace and pomegranate and orange garden outside the windows; it was impossible to picture a more romantic retreat. On the other side of the garden extended a long line of palaces, all exquisite in decoration. He was even given leave to explore the zenana, neglected for a hundred and fifty years and inhabited by monkeys and a few servants. 'The unbroken silence, the glorious view, the fairy-like palace with its Oriental garden, it is impossible to imagine such delightful solitude.' The beauty of the linked palaces was enhanced by the silent ruin of the city spreading about it. An incomparable palace, Bishop Heber called it. . . .

Is the Maharajah who owns Amber as hospitable today? He himself prefers to live in his huge palace in Jaipur; to make Amber a comfortable residence would be costly. All these near-perfect palaces – for Amber is not badly ruined – that strew this enigmatic sub-continent in abandoned beauty, raise the question, why does no prince, plutocrat or government official inhabit them? But it appears that Indians like to keep their abandoned cities and palaces lying empty, decaying slowly in the sun, renounced for ever to monkeys, peacocks and pigeons, museum pieces little heeded. . . .

The beauty of a palace, as of temples, owes much to incidental factors – a large fortress above it, an ancient city below it, a lake holding its image in green water, valleys and hills and woods as background, submerging jungle drowning it, the sea lapping at its feet, or a shadow-green canal against its walls. Any ruin of a palace posed on a small island, or round a lake, as the tumbling palaces of Sarkhej near Ahmedabad are posed; palaces riven by trees, crowned by creepers and blossom, banyan boughs thrusting through carved windows, wild figs and prickly pears springing up through cracks in marble floors, as in the old Deccan city of Bijapur, with its records of dead glory; palaces where princes have feasted and adventurers have intrigued, as in . . . Murshidabad, where Clive and Warren Hastings both inhabited, and that now crumble to desolation – these too are good. All over India such palaces crumble and are beautiful. Almost the most immense in extent, and in the number of separate buildings linked by galleries and courtyards (they covered more ground, it seems, than Versailles and the Tuileries), is Akbar's imperial palace at Fatehpur-Sikri, abandoned after fifteen years. The palace has everything that could be desired . . . Fatehpur must have been such a desirable residence when completed that no one but an Indian Rajah could have deserted it. But Akbar found no difficulty; owing to water troubles he transferred his court to Lahore, and then to Agra, and left his elaborate red stone palace empty but for a few guards. Now it stands deserted; its red buildings, kept bare of encroaching greenery, remind some visitors of a fairy palace, others of barracks.

With many Hindu and Mogul palaces, once of great beauty, the ruin has consisted in vulgar modern destruction and adaptation, such as the British mutilation after the mutiny of Shah Jahan's superb imperial palace in Old Delhi, to make way for barracks. Marble floors and arcaded courts were removed, elegant chambers and courts turned into guard-rooms, brick partitions put up, blocking windows and arcades. . . . The Persian inscription at each end of the Hall of Audience – 'If there is a paradise on the earth's face, it is this, oh it is this, oh it is this' – reads now with a melancholy irony.

Actually, India is set about with abandoned palace paradises. . . . A journey over the deserted palaces of India, savouring in each its nice approximation to, or degree of, ruin, estimating the charm added by desertion and decay and fallen pomp, would be a delicious employ of several years. One can cite a few examples, but all to no purpose; they are to be seen, not heard of. For that is a great point about them, they can be seen, they are nearly all there. Unlike so many palaces elsewhere, of which one gratefully accepts the fragments that remain – here a broken wall, there a portal, a few prostrate pillars, all wholeness gone. . . .

It is . . . the north and centre, and more particularly Rajputana, that abound in palaces. They are beautiful, often built on rocks, over water, often terraced up from solid substructures, sometimes bastioned, nearly always picturesque. Many of the best are unruined, and ineligible for these pages; some have been spoiled by modern alterations. India is not a pride of palaces as she is a holiness of temples and mosques and monasteries: but the best Hindu ruins have the lavishness, the uninhibited glory and intricate richness, the dark and dreaming imagination, that stirs like musky jungle scents in the brooding air of the ancient India, shattered and startled and woken to new forms by the rushing torrents of life from the Saracen north, that blew up domes like bubbles and starred them with bright enamel and laid out immense arcaded palace courts. The Rajahs, Hindu and Mogul, who built and lived in the palaces were lush, beauty-loving monarchs who loved pomps and glories and elephants and dancers and lusts and the decorated scene; over the amazing continent their fabulous palaces in ruin are haunted with all these.

Far more ruined are the great Sassanian palaces, which stand in tremendous and lonely majesty about Mesopotamia and Persia. The most magnificent palace ruin in Mesopotamia is probably Ukheidur by the Euphrates. To some travellers the first sight of it has been the most memorable experience of life.

'It reared its mighty walls out of the sand, almost untouched by time, breaking the long lines of the waste with its huge towers, steadfast and massive, as though it were, as I had first thought, the work of nature, not of man.'

Coming nearer, passing through the great bastioned walls of masonry and brick, one enters huge vaulted halls, smaller vaulted chambers, corridors, and open courts, walls with blind arcades, stairways climbing up three storeys, windowed bastions, fluted domes, arched doors, tiles of brick and stone. Archaeologists cannot date Ukheidur with certainty. Sassanid in style, was it before or soon after the Arab conquest, or as late as the Abbaside period? It has much in common with the Sassanian Firuzabad and Ctesiphon. Probably, therefore, early post-conquest. Whatever its date, it is the most imposing ruin in Mesopotamia; better than Samarra, better than Ctesiphon, because there is so much more of it.

Chosroes I's palace at Ctesiphon, built about 550, of brick, not masonry, on the east bank of the Tigris, opposite the mounds of ancient Seleucia, is a noble fragment, the palace must have been immense, larger than Sarvistan or Firuzabad; all that remains now is the great central vaulted hall and one wall of one wing. The Dieulafoys, seventy years ago, saw the east walls of both wings, and the vault of the hall was still intact. Of all Sassanian buildings except Persepolis, Ctesiphon palace has most renown; less for its present ruin, its huge uncentred vault and carved wall (carving not remarkable, not even good), than for its famous past, the ancient glory of Ctesiphon city, the great Sassanian capital which succeeded Seleucia, the hierarchic grandeur of Chosroes I, the destroyer of Antioch, and the fabulous beauties of the palace as described by its Arab conquerors – the golden throne, the carpet on which Paradise was embroidered in gold and silver and pearls, the great audience hall where the *élite* society of Persia crowded to pay court. . . .

It has been said that only archaeologists see beauty in this architecture, that its interest is historical and architectural, not aesthetic. But the great ruined palaces of Persia impose themselves with a superb strength. These broken domes, great open vestibules, long façades with engaged arcades, great blocks of brick or grey stone, tremendous thick walls, barrel-vaulted rooms, Sassanian carvings – they make their effect rather by mass than detail. Ardashir's great third-century palace at Firuzabad, with its tremendous ruin-littered courts and domes, chambers, and its approximations to Romanesque, Byzantine and Moslem, would never be called exquisite, it has a kind of elaborate, magnificent clumsiness; but, standing above that sad landscape and the ruined city, towered over by two castles, it is hugely ghostly and

impressive. The Dieulafoys were awestruck by the immense vaulted structure, *'que n'embellit aucun décor'*. The vast halls, the enormous arches, the linked chambers of the harem, the domes, the open courts strewn with broken masonry, stood in a plain littered with the remains of a dead city; in front of its great vestibule an artificial lake lay among shards and fragments of stone parapets. It was all, Madame Dieulafoy found, *'triste au possible'*, and engendered the melancholy usual in those who survey ruins so long abandoned to the devastations of men and time. . . . Robert Byron, fifty years after the learned Dieulafoys, was interested in the place of the palace in the development of architecture; his account of it is the best we have. . . .

After these huge Sassanian affairs, the small ruined brick palaces that strew Persia, mud melting back into the soil, seem ephemeral, fragile, charming, set in gardens that will in the end grow over their remains. When they are perished, there will be no digging them up, they will be one with the earth. Not like the Abbaside eighth-century palaces now being dug piece by piece, out of Jericho. Nor like the marble palaces fallen broken about Italy, their slabs, sunk deep in vineyards and olive gardens, dug up by *contadini* and carried in creaking carts by oxen to builders' yards to find their places in cemeteries, in churches, in new palazzi and villas on the hills, persisting through time and change and mortal chance.

Palaces should be exquisite in death, like the Porphyrogenitus palace in the walls of Byzantium, like the Blachernae palace in the northern corner of the city, like the great chain of imperial palaces disintegrating through the centuries in its western tip. Or like the small ruined palaces that stand in decay in formal grottoed gardens and parks about South Germany and Austria, or the great disintegrating palaces of Russian noblemen, mouldering and discoloured beside artificial lakes, green with weed, used for stables and agricultural implements and lodgings for workers, the windows fallen in. Or the sombrely truculent baronial fortified palaces that range down Italy from north to south and from east to west: castles or palaces, the distinction is nice, they served for both. Or, more delicate, more palatial, the for ever dying, for ever vanishing palaces of China; or the broken-domed Byzantine shells with their dim fading wall paintings where the Despots reigned on Greek hills. . . .

In ruined palaces there lies peculiar pleasure. The grandeur they had, the courtly life led in them, the banquets, the music, the dancing, the painted walls, the sculptures, the rich tapestries, the bright mosaics, the princely chatter, the foreign envoys coming and going, the merchants laying their costly bales before the royal treasurer – and now the shattered walls, the broken columns, the green trees thrusting through the crumbling floors. Fallen pride, wealth and fine living in the dust, the flitting shades of patrician ghosts, the silence where imperious voices rang, the trickle of unchannelled springs where fountains soared, of water where wine flowed. All this makes for that melancholy delight so eagerly sought, so gratefully treasured, by man in his brief passage down the corridor of time, from which, looking this way and that, he may observe such enchanting chambers of the past.

Spalato, Yugoslavia. Peristyle of the Palace of Diocletian

209 Spalato, Yugoslavia. Peristyle of the Palace of Diocletian
Medieval houses peep incongruously through the giant colonnades of a Roman palace. The retreat which Diocletian built for himself at Spalato at the beginning of the fourth century was divided into four by two arcaded streets crossing each other at the centre. At the end of the southern arm was the entrance portico (seen here in the left of the photograph) to the Great Hall.

210 Tivoli Vecchio, Italy. Statue of Nilus at Hadrian's Villa
Statues representing the river Nile holding a cornucopia of fruits to symbolize its fertility were popular with Roman collectors. Hadrian went further—his Canopus had to evoke the actual atmosphere of Egypt (see below). At the other end of the canal is a system of underground rooms ending in a shrine to Serapis.

211 Tivoli Vecchio, Italy. The Canopus of Hadrian's Villa
Swans float and mutilated statues raise their arms across the silent pleasure grounds of Tivoli near Rome, the wish-fulfilment dream of an emperor's old age. The pool in the background is one of the many features by which Hadrian attempted to reconstruct in miniature the world of his memories. 'To its different parts', wrote the Roman historian Spartianus, 'he assigned the names of celebrated buildings and localities, such as the Lyceum, the Prytaneum, the Canopus, the Stoa Poecile and Tempe.' The real Canopus was a valley in Egypt connected by a canal with Alexandria and containing an ancient temple to Serapis. Egypt had poignant associations for Hadrian—it was in the waters of the Nile that his young favourite Antinous had been so mysteriously drowned.

212 Amber, India. Palace of Man Singh I
The seventeenth-century gardens of the Maharajas of Amber (gardens, like buildings, have their ruins) were among the wonders of India. They are now barely recognizable, but are being carefully restored. With their intricate and artificial patterns, zigzags, star-shapes, ornamental pools and bridges, they are thought to have had some influence on the Baroque garden of Europe.

213 Amber, India. Wall decoration from the Palace of Man Singh I
'Ever-present screens of marble tracery' seemed to Kipling part of the atmosphere of Amber—heavy with luxury but faintly sinister.

214 Ctesiphon, Iraq. Palace of Shapur I
The great brick vault of Ctesiphon, covering a span of 83 feet, is one of the triumphs of ancient engineering, equalling even the achievements of Roman and Byzantine architects. The façade follows the same scheme as the Palace of Firuzabad (Plate 219), but is conceived on a far grander scale. The way the vault is constructed can clearly be seen in the photograph. Its lower courses are laid horizontally, each layer projecting slightly beyond the one below. Above that (about a third of the way up) the courses change to vertical

and become true arches exerting a diagonal thrust. At the end of the hall a door in the high south wall led into the state rooms of the palace. Scholars are still not agreed about its date; it probably belongs to the reign of Ardashir's son and successor Shapur I (AD 241–72), but parts of it may be later.

215 Ukheidur, Iraq. Palace of Isa Ibn Musa
The lonely palace of Ukheidur lies in the parched Iraqi desert about seventy-five miles south-west of Baghdad. Its high fortified walls (62 feet, including the now destroyed battlements) enclose a large rectangle of which the palace proper, set against the north wall, occupied less than half. This view is taken from one of the openings in the north wall, just east of the main north gate. In the foreground are the ruins of the palace—the Court of Honour, the Great Hall and other luxurious apartments, now only crumbling rubble—and beyond them the courtyard, the south fortification wall and the south gate.

216–17 Ukheidur, Iraq. Palace of Isa Ibn Musa
Seen from the north-west. To the right is the west front. All four sides look almost identical—twelve semicircular towers dividing the wall into eleven bays, each consisting of two big niches at the bottom and four arrow-slits at the top (these can be seen from the inside in Plate 215). On the left is a building of similar design, now called the Northern Annexe, but its purpose is unknown; it lies outside the main rectangle of walls. The palace itself probably owes its existence to Isa Ibn Musa, the nephew of Caliph al-Mansur, who came here in AD 774, but its history is a blank.

218 Firuzabad, Iran. Palace of Ardashir
Camels scratch for a few blades of grass where once a populous city stood. Here the first Sassanian king Ardashir built his capital of Firuzabad (mid-third century AD). It was planned—like the cities of the Parthians whom Ardashir had just defeated in the great battle of Susiana (AD 224)—as a perfect circle, with a fire-temple in the exact centre. Outside the boundary he built his palace (seen here in the distance)—now almost the only reminder of Firuzabad's glory.

219 Firuzabad, Iran. Palace of Ardashir
The palace consisted of a large central arch leading into a tunnel-like recess, flanked by symmetrical walls patterned by niches, and all originally covered with stucco. Farther back, and visible in the photograph, three domed halls, the central one entered by the door at the end of the tunnel.

220 Constantinople, Turkey. Palace of Constantine Porphyrogenitus
This is the only fragment now standing above ground of the vast palace of the Byzantine emperors which once amazed visitors from every corner of the earth. This façade formed one side of an inner courtyard. The ground storey is an open colonnade; the two upper storeys are encrusted with variegated marble and coloured brickwork. In date it probably belongs to the early tenth century, the reign of

Constantine VII Porphyrogenitus ('Born to the Purple'). On the right is part of the city's massive defence system, begun by Constantine and strengthened by emperor after emperor, which enabled it to hold out against attack from east and west—Turks and Goths, Moslem and barbarian—for over 1000 years.

221 Jericho, Israel. Window from the Khirbet al-Mafjar
This window—a stone knot with six interlaced ribbons forming a six-pointed star within a circle—is one of the most beautiful inventions of Islamic art. Ninety-six of the hundred and six stones that composed it were found scattered at the bottom of a stair-well and the whole window has been patiently fitted together like a jigsaw puzzle by the archaeologists. It is over 6 feet in diameter and probably occupied the middle of a gable overlooking the western side of the central courtyard. Khirbet al-Mafjar was a country mansion of the Umayyad establishment about a mile and a half north of Jericho and was built between A D 725 and 750.

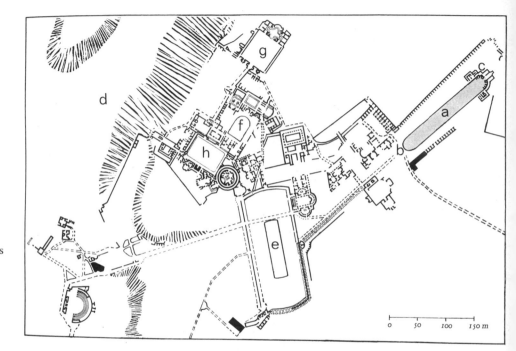

TIVOLI VECCHIO
Hadrian's Villa
a   Canopus
b   Nilus, arcade and statues
c   Shrine of Serapis
d   Vale of Tempe
e   Stoa Poecile
f   Imperial Palace
g   Piazza d'Oro
h   Court of the Libraries

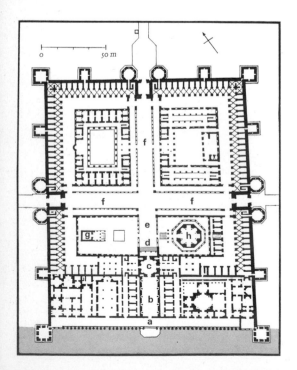

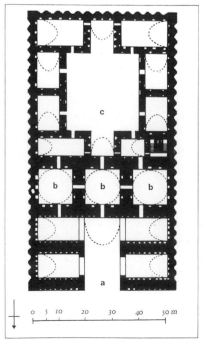

SPALATO (far left)
Palace of Diocletian
a   Gallery facing the sea
b   Central hall of the Emperor's apartments
c   Vestibule
d   Portico with sphinx
e   Peristyle (southern arm of four streets)
f   Colonnaded streets
g   Temple of Jupiter
h   Emperor's Mausoleum

FIRUZABAD (left)
Palace of Ardashir
a   Arched recess
b   Domed halls
c   Courtyard surrounded by residential quarters

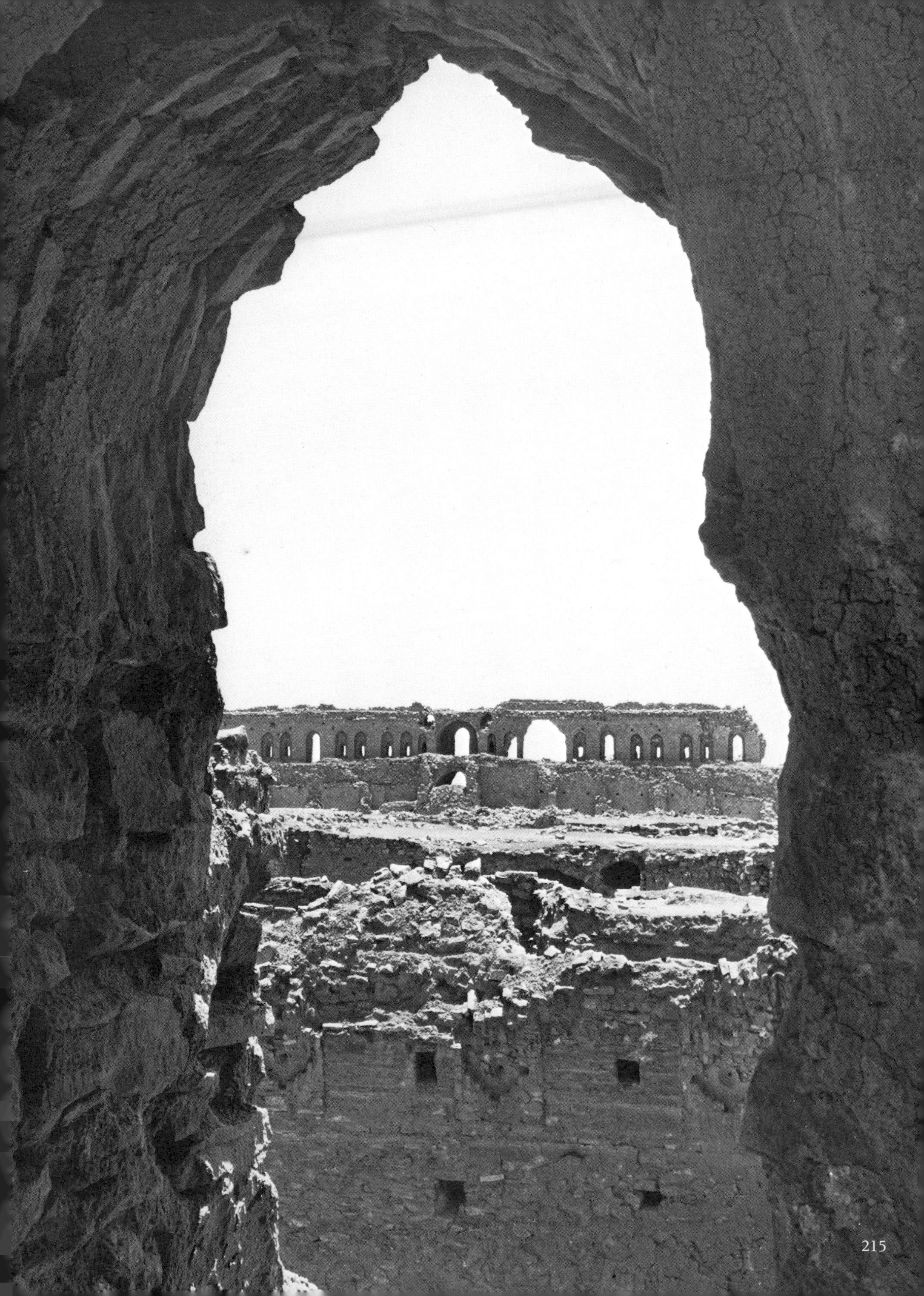

V A fantasy of castles

The castle has always been a formidable image, a powerful intimidating fantasy of the human imagination. The fortress, the citadel, the craggy tower dominating the landscape: it is older than history, as natural to man as the eyrie to the eagle. To defend oneself, to attack others, to live in guarded pride: these are its laudable aims. Until they are ruined, no one but their owners, and those who live under their protection, has liked them; once they are shattered and dismantled, admiration supervenes; they become pets, the most esteemed ruined objects in a landscape, curdling the blood with awe, delighting the soul with majestic beauty.

> *Bless'd too is he who, midst his tufted trees,*
> *Some ruin'd castle's lofty towers sees,*
> *Imbosom'd high upon the mountain's brow,*
> *Or nodding o'er the stream that glides below . . .*

said Payne Knight, voicing the general view of his generation. Looking on these formidable shattered piles, men have been stirred to high moral reflections; they have thought on retribution, on the wickedness and pride natural to those who inhabit castles, and on the ruin into which they have now fallen. 'High castles which held many gluttons and thieves stand and teach that fierce gentlemen do not reign long.' And,

> *Beneath these battlements, within those walls,*
> *Power dwelt amidst her passions; in proud state*
> *Each robber chief upheld his armed halls,*
> *Doing his evil will. . . .*

But see what happened to him:

> *Though to the clouds his castle seem'd to climb,*
> *And frown'd defiance to the desperate foe,*
> *Though deem'd invincible, the conqueror, Time,*
> *Levell'd the fabric, as the founder, low. . . .*

> *Though his rich hours in revelry were spent,*
> *With Comus and the laughter-loving crew,*
> *And the sweet brow of Beauty, still unbent,*
> *Brighten'd his fleecy moments as they flew. . . .*

Happy baron, one likes to think that he led this amiable and Sybaritish life before he was levelled with his fabric.

But, looking on the fortresses that strew all lands, craggy stumps, fierce battlemented towers, mighty walls with loophole windows suitable for guns and for boiling oil, huge sprawls of enceintes, massive curtain walls, moats, drawbridges, vaulted halls, winding turret stairs, and all the rest of the castle paraphernalia, one feels that Comus and his crew would have had short shrift, and that the chieftain's moments were probably on the whole less fleecy than bloody. Such appears to have been the opinion of the Portuguese exile poet, Almeida Garrett, who, surveying Dudley Castle, saw nothing but the foolish débris of fallen leaves, the fallen walls that choked the moat, and the imagined corpses of those who had perished fighting through the pride or whim of the domineering baron. Garrett took the dark view of castles.

Castles, like temples and churches, have always been reproductive: they generate new castles on their foundations, broken walls, and razed sites. Since all things must have a beginning, one must assume that, where the remains of each castle stand or lie, there was once a first castle: but it was probably prehistoric, a pile of stones and earth without form. It was ruined or taken or merely fell down; on its site and fragments rose a new castle, some cyclopean mass, presently to be ruined in its turn, to make way for massive walls and fortified gates and to move into the recognizable history of two and three thousand years BC. How many citadels lie, ruin on ruin, on the site of Troy? How many lie below Mycenae and Tiryns and Phaestos? What fortresses preceded all those forts that command and menace the strategic points of Attica, looking across the mountains at Athens as Phyle does? In the massive fort of Phyle with its circular tower, Thrasybulus, expelled from Athens by the Thirty Tyrants, settled with seventy-eight martial comrades, looking at Hymettus, Athens, and the Saronic Gulf, and sallied forth to capture the Piraeus and send the Tyrants packing. This is what we think of when we look up at Phyle's walls. For all castles hold their stories. All these kastros, palaeokastros, acropolises guarded by their broken fragments of ancient wall, that stand, battered sentinels, like Eleutherae that guards the pass of Kithaeron, about the mountains and islands of Greece, all the Roman castles of the Campagna, the Volscian and Sabine hills, all the dead Etruscan cities, the castles of southern Italy and of the Trentino, all the Roman-Byzantine-Arab-Frankish castles that ennoble the crags and seaports of Syria, Anatolia, Cyprus and Rhodes, and the desolate mountains of Mesopotamia, all the great Norman and Edwardian castles of Britain, the incomparable medieval castles and Renaissance châteaux of France, the Hohenstaufen palace-castles with which Frederick II decorated and defended Puglia, the dramatic *Schlösser* above the foaming rivers of Germany, the castle ruins that moulder proudly on the hilltops of Spain, on the lonely precipices and gorges of the ancient Armenian kingdom of Cilicia, Byzantine forts along the orcharded Crimean shores, Anatolian fastnesses, Abruzzi mountain citadels guarding tumbling brown stone villages as ruined as themselves – every one of these has its story and its drama: they are what Anthony Wood would have called 'romancey'. Here, in those ruined robber-baron keeps that the powerful Roman families and their Gothic invaders threw up in the Colosseum, the Palatine, the tombs, the great baths, any ruin ready to their hand, all about Rome and the Campagna from the fifth century to the fifteenth, the story of feudal Rome was bloodily enacted, the Orsini, the Colonna, the Barberini and the rest waged their wars and fought their feuds, hanged their foes and feasted their friends, broke their pledges and slew their wives.

These broken fortresses seem to brood, darkly sinister, looming out of a lurid past. Few are beautiful with the beauty of the medieval castles of Britain and France, the crusaders' castles of the east, the Gothic ruins of Germany; they have the sullen lowering of the defeated bully, and the high provenance of Rome englamours them. All over Italy the feudal castles stand, some almost intact, most shattered or decayed: you may scarcely see a little town of any antiquity which has not its ruined castle gaping blindly down on it. Their histories are only worth examining by those with a great relish for animated slaughter and intrigue; one looks instead at the poise of their broken walls against the backcloth of olive-grey and pine-green mountain above the pink-washed town and the little stone-jettied port of fishing-boats. The castles, like the towns and ports and mountain villages, are part of the furniture of the mind, they belong to the earliest fairy stories, perhaps to the oldest ancestral memories. In the imaginations of Gothic and Celtic northerners, the most deeply rooted fantasy is the Gothic castle. There they tower on their crags above rivers and lakes, the ruined dwellings of the wicked barons, a few turrets left, or high keeps and battlemented walls, posed ready for the artist, dramatically excessive, satisfying food for the *ruinenhungrige Phantasie* of the nostalgic mind. . . .

Or, if one prefers dignified landscape to the lizard and the speckled toad, one can say, with Dorothy Wordsworth, 'What a dignity does the form of an ancient castle or tower confer upon a precipitous woody or craggy eminence!' But the imagination is stormed by the ruin itself: castle after castle rides crag after crag like battleships riding a high sea: Godesberg, Drachenfels, Falkenburg, Scarborough, Tintagel, Rhuddlan, Corfe, Gaillard, Coucy, a hundred more such melodramatic visions startle the eyes and haunt the soul. The castled mind is confirmed in its credulous dreams, in its dark aspirations and fears. This is the reality that runs, stealthy and secret, a dark subliminal river, below the threshold of awareness. These are what man, out of some deep need, throws up everywhere that he inhabits; these are what man, in anger and fear, destroys, so that the world is like a fantasy of tumbling towers by Monsù Desiderio. Everywhere *châteaux disparus, verfallene Schlösser, castelli rovinati*, castles in ruin. . . .

Castles are seldom indigenous. They are apt to be built in apprehensive aggression by conquerors – the Normans in Britain, the Romans and Byzantines all over their far-flung empires. It was the Byzantine emperors, the Franks, and the Venetians who threw up the great defensive mountain and sea castles of Cyprus. Of these the hugest and the most dramatic is St Hilarion, built by the Byzantines on a monastery site in the Kyrenia mountains. Twisting up and up into the sky, terrace above terrace, tower over tower, till it ends in an eyrie that surveys the world, it is a dramatic pile of ruin, rocks, and wild aromatic trees and shrubs springing out of them. Strengthened by the Lusignans, besieged by Frederick II during his assaults on Cyprus, it became a palace of the Lusignan kings; dismantled by the wary Venetians, it is now a vast towered enceinte, a picture-book castle for elf kings, sprawling over two twin crests with its maze of gate-houses, courts, arches, kitchens, cisterns, church, vaulted chambers and halls, terraces, and steep flights of grass-grown steps. Even wilder and more ruinous and haunting the verges of dream is Kantara, a smaller castle in the mountain range to the north-east, a broken labyrinth of ruin on a dizzying precipice high above the distant green-blue sea that curves into the indented coast. Less a show-place than Hilarion, it is still more utterly a ruined place, given over to desolation. Difficult and fatiguing of access, it is, as the British consul in Aleppo complained, really very much 'out of repair'. Most of the other Cyprus castles are more tranquil of approach. . . .

The ruined castles of England, Scotland, Wales and Ireland stand, a chain of stony splendour, linking together the fierce epochs of our Celtic, Roman, Saxon, Danish, Norman and English races. There are Norman keeps built within Roman walls, great clusters of massive round Norman towers, square towers and battlemented walls rearing themselves on steep heights, towered enceintes rising above a lilied moat in sham perfection, as at Bodiam, where all within the walls is ruin; wild and jagged arches and battlements cresting grassy Dorset hills, or climbing Cornish cliffs above a beating green sea, single round towers standing like funnels all over Ireland, tremendous shattered masses, tree-grown, frowning grandly down on the Border country below, guarding the Scottish firths, defending the Welsh ports, dominating the walled cities and cathedrals; small castles on islands, fortified manor houses of timber and stone. There are many hundreds of British ruined castles, and such is British affection for them that in front of each someone or other, and often a whole charabanc, is picnicking, while others climb the walls and towers with cameras. Nothing but the seaside gives our island race, of high and low degree, a keener pleasure. When we say 'a ruin', it is, in childhood, normally a castle that we mean. Henry James thought it was the sense of the past that we like in them: 'the sensation of dropping back personally into the past . . . while I lay on the grass beside the well in the little sunny court of this small castle' (Stokesay) 'and lazily appreciated the still definite details of medieval life. The place is a capital example of a small *gentilhommière* of the thirteenth century.' And so up the corkscrew staircase of the tower 'to the most charming part of every old castle . . . the bright dizzy platform at the tower-top'.

It may be the past that we seek, or the power, the glory and the romance, or the catastrophe of wreckage, or merely the wonder and the grandeur of a dwelling so unlike our own. Some have had the pleasure of digging out wrecked castles gone to earth, restoring and putting them together, uncovering moats, walls and nutteries from a wilderness of briars and weeds, making there a dwelling and a garden, as at Sissinghurst in Kent. Others have, as the romantic ruin-visitors of the eighteenth and nineteenth centuries found, made their homes among the towers, built their hovels in the walls. . . .

Sometimes ruins have been intentionally manufactured by destruction, not in anger or in arson, but in aesthetic enthusiasm. In 1836 Mr Hussey, the grandfather of the present owner of Scotney Castle in Kent, moved by this enthusiasm and desirous of building himself a new and more commodious house to live in, abandoned his ancient fortified manor house by the lilied moat, the tower surviving from the fourteenth-century castle. . . . Mr Hussey had a fine new house quarried out of the hillside high above the old castle; and, in order to see from his windows a picturesque object, had . . . the old house partially and fashionably ruined . . . the walls shattered into jagged roughness

at the top. He achieved his picturesque object; from the first it must have been beautiful; today, creeper-grown and the colour of lichen, standing with the grey and rust-coloured barbicaned castle tower against a steep wilderness of quarry flowers behind, and at its foot the lily moat reflecting sky, trees, tower and ruined mansion, today it makes an exquisite picture. If ever ruin-making has justified itself, this has; the scene has a harmonious grace, the grace achieved in greater or less measure by many time-struck or fate-struck ruins, and by few shams. . . . As a ruin, however, this delightful . . . fortress barely qualifies. We must leave it for the more shattered remains that castle the perhaps over-castled earth.

Yes, there are too many. Crusader castles, Byzantine castles, Arab castles in deserts, such as the immense (too immense) Qasr el Haïr in the Palmyrene desert, the picturesque decorated Qasr built in the Roman acropolis above Amman, Masada on the Dead Sea, Kerak in Moab, some hundreds more scattered about Syria and Judaea. . . .

All about Syria and Palestine they stand, the crusaders' castles we call them, but really also Phoenician, Greek, Roman, Byzantine, and Arab in succession; upon the site the stones were piled and used by each occupier in turn; the crusaders built their great fortresses on ancient towns, taking their columns and stones for foundations; at Byblos the Frankish castle rose out of the Roman theatre. But usually castle grew out of castle, and the Byzantine and Saracen forts that strewed Syria became Latin-French castles, built by the same Greek and Syrian builders. Through each phase the antique Roman columns and stones often sustained the foundations, and still are to be seen. When the crusaders, expelled from their last stronghold in the Holy Land, sailed for Cyprus, the fortresses they left behind were seized and held by Saracens, later to be turned into homes for whole villages. Their *magnum opus*, Crac des Chevaliers . . . that huge fastness of great concentric towered walls, vaulted halls, granaries, store-rooms, stables, chapel, standing high on a spur of rock to be seen across many miles of wild landscape, that jewel in the superb stone chain that the crusaders strung across Syria, had grown from a small Arab castle into a mighty citadel, nearly a city. Almost impregnable, it fell at last to Sultan Beibars in 1271. It was not much ruined; Beibars occupied it, and after him other rulers; later, the Arab population moved in; Crac became a village, full of peasants, cattle, asses, camels, goats and poultry. The Romanesque chapel was turned into a mosque, the great decorated hall and gallery were built over with small houses or used as stables. Better houses were built above, the summits of the walls being knocked down to provide stones. In 1895 its state was horrible – the glory of the Knights Hospitallers was a peasant village, *'croupissant sur son fumier'*, freshly mutilated yearly, defiled with the ordure of years; the whole lower storey of the second enceinte was covered in dirt, flung down by dwellers on the first floor through holes in the vaulted ceiling. Kala'at el Husn, the Arabs have called it; when Gertrude Bell visited it early this century its topmost tower was inhabited by the Kaimakam, who hospitably entertained her in a guest chamber of the tower: she has recorded the pleasures of a guest in Crac; the coming at sunset on a stormy evening to the Dark Tower, riding through a splendid Arab gateway into a vaulted corridor built over a winding stair, till at last they came into the courtyard in the centre of the keep, where a crowd of village inhabitants surrounded them and the Kaimakam took Miss Bell up the tower to the guest room and an evening of polite hospitality. Next morning:

'I explored the castle from end to end, with immense satisfaction to the eternal child that lives in the soul of all of us and takes more delight in the dungeons and battlements of a fortress than in any other relic of antiquity. Kala'at el Husn is so large that half of the population of the village is lodged in the vaulted substructures of the keep, while the garrison occupies the upper towers. . . . The keep contained a chapel, now converted into a mosque, and a banquet hall with Gothic windows, the tracery of which was blocked with stones to guard those who dwelt within against the cold.'

The internal decoration was Gothically exquisite; and Miss Bell does not mention dirt; perhaps the castle had lately been spring-cleaned. But the real cleaning began with the French, who took over in 1929 and set in hand the gigantic work of clearance, eviction and repair.

Now Crac is tidied and restored to a cleaner magnificence than it can have enjoyed since the Hospitallers moved in; it looks what it is, the finest medieval monument in Syria, impressive, beautiful and stupendous, a glorious showpiece; but it no longer looks a ruin. One would have liked to have seen it thirty years ago, with its village of peasants and livestock incongruously swarming in those beautiful halls. . . .

In a land of ruined castles, of all periods and types, it is the crusader castles that perhaps most stir our imaginations. That extraordinary, valiant long adventure in conquest, exotic colonization, missionary Christianity spread by the sword in the land that bore it, western chivalry transplanted, more strangely, into the alien east – the whole affair has, it had nine centuries ago, the picturesque quality that excites; its massive ruins, flung about the Levant with such prodigal magnificence, capture us as castles more indigenous less wholly do. . . .

Castles, by common consent, should be ruined: Corfe, Loches, Gaillard, San Felice Circeo, all the romantic castles of Italy and its mountainous islands, and of Southern France, are more intriguing to most people than Windsor and the châteaux on the Loire, a Salvator Rosa castle on a precipice than the unflawed circle of St Angelo on the Tiber, a Drachenfels than a restored Lutherolatrous Wartburg. A little ruin is best; not so much as wholly to destroy the form; a touch of ruin, such as has romanticized the remarkable chain of the Hohenstaufen castles in Puglia with which Frederick II guarded his south Italian estates and in which he took his pleasures. There, surrounded by *conforts modernes* (or rather, returning, amid Gothic barbarism, to the *conforts anciens* of imperial Rome) the Stupor Mundi took his Sunday bath, hunted and hawked, and watched the habits of birds. In the largest of them, Lucera, he kept leopards, eunuchs, a harem, and so many Saracens that the city of Lucera was named Lucera Saracenorum; one may still see the remains of the mosque in the castle, as well as of the tall octagonal palace tower. All the castles are damaged, by the assaults of time, man and the heaving earth; looking at Lucera on its hill, one expects leopards, devouring plump eunuchs and urged on by Saracens, to bound out of the broken gateways.

Ruin also adds enormously to the huge Byzantine-Turkish castles that tower on both sides of the Bosphorus, each a climbing pile of round towers and battlemented walls running steeply down to the water's edge, with Turkish houses clustering in their shelter. Built by the Byzantine emperors for defence, they were added to and strengthened by the Turks after the taking of Constantinople; the enormous Roumeli Hissar, standing on a precipitous hill on the Europe shore, with its twelfth-century 'Towers of Lethe' and its Turkish wall of 1452; the smaller Anadoli Hissar opposite on the Asia shore, the jaggedly ruined Hieron on the same. The shattered magnificence of these Bosphorus castles conveys the grandeur of Byzantium, and the tenacious Ottoman hold on its conquests; they have the palatial touch, the air of finery, which the crusader and Sicilian castles lack; they suggest the exotic potentate, as King Christophe's tremendous castle towering on the heights above his Haiti palace suggests it, and the extraordinary impregnable fortress of Daulatabad in Hyderabad, and Kala-i-Dukhtar rearing in terraced splendour its precipice-built walls at Firuzabad, and the twisted eye-catcher of Georgian Tiflis.

All these castles in ruin, and a thousand more, climb, a composite fantasy of castelry, about the hills and valleys and winding roads of the mind. They give no security: they are shattered, shot-riddled, they crumble before our eyes. The drawbridges are down, the keep will fall: there is no security, which is what we always knew. Yet still the castles climb the dark crags.

Dorset, England. Great Keep of Corfe Castle, twelfth century

229 Syria. Crac des Chevaliers

The Inner Ward of Crac lay in the centre of a mighty system of fortifications which still arouses wonder. This photograph is taken looking north from the upper court of the Inner Ward (marked *d* on the plan on p. 228). The visitor to the castle (or the enemy if he had forced his way so far) enters through an arch underneath the masonry on the right (*e*). On his right (centre of the photograph, *f*) he has the arch of a vestibule leading to the chapel (*g*). In front of him (*h*) is an arcade of traceried windows like a cloister, with a door in the middle that led through into the Great Hall (*j*). The stairs at the back (*k*) ascend to the inner ramparts. Crac consisted of two circles of walls separated by a ditch partially filled with water. The inner circle was virtually another castle inside the first, and could only be entered by passing an extraordinary series of obstacles—an entrance gate (*a*), a narrow passage that doubles back on itself (*b*) and several more doors, portcullises and exposed positions where missiles could be dropped from above.

Crac was one of the headquarters of the Knights Hospitallers, a military order dedicated, like the Templars, to the defence of the Holy Land. It guarded the vital passes over the mountains from the east to the Mediterranean coast, and was the scene of continual battle and bloodshed for the 150 years of its history, being finally abandoned by the Knights, after withstanding many attacks, in 1271.

230 Lazio, Italy. Roccasinibalda Castle

The fine Renaissance palace-castle of Roccasinibalda ('ròcca' means a fortified hill-top), about thirty miles north-east of Rome, was begun in the early 1530s by Cardinal Alessandro Cesarini. His architect is said to have been the famous Baldassare Peruzzi, one of the leading figures of the Roman High Renaissance, but if so he died before much progress on the building could have been made. The most striking feature about it is visible only from the air—its plan is based on a heraldic eagle, with bastions and terraces outlining the beak, tail and outspread wings. In the seventeenth century the last of the Cesarini, Livia Cesarini, married into the Sforza family and the castle passed into their possession.

231 Cyprus. St Hilarion Castle

From the Lower Ward of the castle, itself a heavily defended position, the attacker was faced by a yet more impregnable fortress, the summit of the mountain, or Upper Ward. In the centre, clinging to the spur of rock, is the tower known as Prince John's Tower, 'the donjon-tower where the great precipice is', as an old chronicler describes it. In 1373 this was the scene of a grisly incident. Prince John of Antioch, who had conspired to assassinate his brother, the previous king of Cyprus, Peter I, held the castle with the aid of a faithful band of Bulgarian mercenaries. But Queen Eleanor, the dead king's widow, persuaded him that they were plotting to murder him, and he summoned them one by one to the top of this tower and had them thrown into the

yawning chasm below. By this act of folly he deprived himself of his best guards and was soon himself murdered by order of the Queen.

Prince John and King Peter were members of the royal Lusignan family, who had ruled Cyprus since the beginning of the thirteenth century. But the earliest buildings at St Hilarion are much older than this. The saint himself was apparently a hermit, otherwise unknown to fame, who with hundreds of others sought refuge in Cyprus when the Holy Land was overrun by the Arabs. Later a Byzantine monastery was built on the site (parts of it remain), and in the eleventh century, when the threat from the Seljuk Turks became serious, the whole stronghold was fortified. The basic plan of the Castle must then have been much as it is now, but most of the buildings visible today date from the reign of the Lusignans. The tower on the left in the photograph is part of the twelfth-century ramparts, built on Byzantine foundations.

232–3 Shropshire, England. Stokesay Castle

Across the still waters of its now peaceful moat, Stokesay Castle has little of the grimness that we should expect from its date and its position next to the Welsh border. The North Tower (left in the photograph) is the oldest part, 1270–80; next came the Great Hall, where the four tall windows (visible under a branch of the tree) are something of a surprise—how could the Lord of Stokesay, John de Verdon, risk these large openings in the outer wall of his castle with apparently no protection other than the moat? The ground on this side is swampy and he must have considered it safe enough. But the next owner, Laurence de Ludlow (John de Verdon went on a Crusade in 1290 and sold Stokesay), evidently decided to take no chances, and built a very strong castellated tower at the south end (on the right). At that time a nobleman needed the King's permission before he could fortify his house with battlements. We know that Laurence de Ludlow received this permission in 1291; his battlements still stand.

234 Sicily, Erice

Perched on the top of a limestone precipice that has been eroded by the wind until it too seems like an ancient work of man, the medieval castle of Erice commands the spacious valleys of northern Sicily from Trapani eastwards towards Palermo. Erice is the Eryx of the Greek and Roman world, the site of a famous temple to Venus ('Venus Erycina'). During the Middle Ages the summit of the cliff was fortified and occupied by most of the races that struggled for the mastery of the island. Parts of the old castle were in use as a prison as late as thirty years ago.

235 Byblos, Lebanon. The Frankish Castle

The only entrance to the squat, square keep of Byblos was across a ditch cut in the rock by the Crusaders who built it. Byblos (which the Crusaders called Giblet) had been captured by Hugues de Lambriac in 1109, and the castle dates from soon after his conquest. The doorway shown here, however, has been reconstructed comparatively recently (note the joggled stones that make up the arch). In the lower courses of the wall the circular stones are of interest—they are probably the ends of antique columns which the Crusaders were in the habit of using, laid flat and at right angles to the surface, to bond their masonry more firmly together.

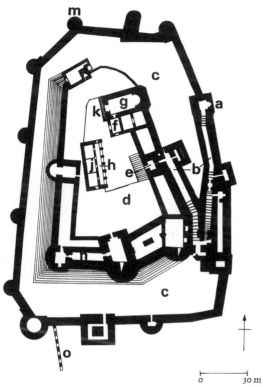

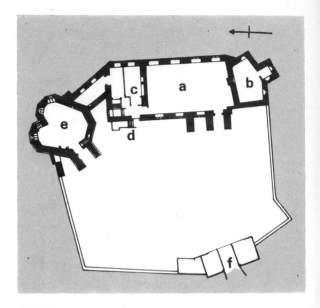

STOKESAY CASTLE

a Great Hall
b North Tower
c Undercroft of Solar
d Stairs to Solar
e South Tower
f Gate-House (Tudor)

CRAC DES CHEVALIERS

a Entrance
b Passage
c Outer Ward
d Inner Ward
e Entrance to Inner Ward
f Vestibule
g Chapel
h Gallery
j Great Hall
k Stairs
m Windmill tower
n Grand Master's lodging
o Aqueduct

ST HILARION CASTLE

a Lower Ward
b Upper Ward
c Prince John's Tower
d One of the rampart towers
e Byzantine church
f Royal Apartments

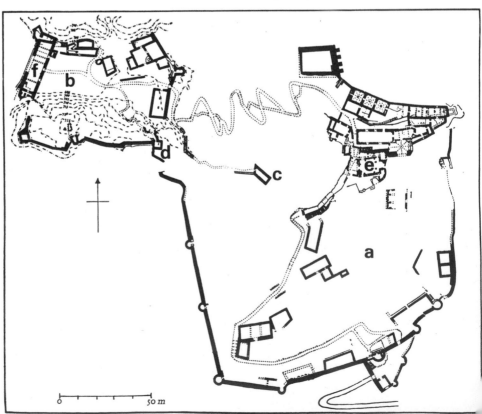

Epilogue

The human race is, and has always been, ruin-minded. The literature of all ages has found beauty in the dark and violent forces, physical and spiritual, of which ruin is one symbol. The symbols change; the need does not. Oedipus, Clytemnestra, Atreus, Medea, children slain and served up in pies to their parents, all the atrocious horrors of Greek drama, of Seneca, of Dante's hell, of Tasso, of the Elizabethans and Jacobeans – these have a profoundly ruinous and welcome gloom, far greater than that of the romantic ruined towers, the bats, toads and ghosts that were so fashionable in eighteenth-century poetry. Shakespeare, Marlowe, Webster, Ford, have all the properties – mass murder, torture, rape, loathsome dungeons and caves, haunted castles, minatory ghosts, witches, blasted heaths, blindings, madness, owls and flitting bats, adders and speckled toads, monstrous passions, suicide, revenge; it is indeed a ruined and ruinous world they inhabit and portray, and no eighteenth-century ruin-poet can hold a candle to them. The ghastly owl shrieks his baleful note in both; the horrid worms twine about the cold corpse in the mouldering grave; there was not much that the later century could add.

What it did add was a kind of cheerful enjoyment of the dismal scene, a brisk, approving gaiety, expressed in firm octosyllabic or decasyllabic lines, with satisfied enumerations of the gloomy objects perceived; and a good moral at the end, as in Dyer's *Grongar Hill*. . . .

As the century proceeded, fashionable gloom increased. By 1745 it was a mode which young poets adopted with fervour . . . ruin, horror, gloom, adders, toads, bats, screech-owls, ivy, wasted towers, Gothic romance, multiplied cheerfully, in poetry, prose and paint. The vast ruined vaults of Piranesi soared before nostalgic eyes; the dark roads stretched back to a formidably romantic past that haunted the mind, an escape from the utilitarian present; before the century's end there was to be Goethe, innumerable writers of Gothic romances, and Hubert Robert of the Ruins, who saw little else worth his painting, and even put the Louvre into picturesque wreckage, as Joseph Gandy later put the Bank of England. Painters, poets, novelists and the general public had come to express articulately what they had from the earliest times unconsciously felt – that

there's a fascination frantic
in a ruin that's romantic.

Should they desire to know why, Diderot could tell them. He exhorted Robert (one would think unnecessarily) to realize that ruins have a poetry of their own. 'You don't know', he said, 'why ruins give so much pleasure. I will tell you. . . . Everything dissolves, everything perishes, everything passes, only time goes on. . . . How old the world is. I walk between two eternities. . . . What is my existence in comparison with this crumbling stone?'

Be that as it may, the realization of mortality does seem to have been the dominant emotion to which ruins then led; or possibly it was only the emotion best understood.

Today we are perhaps more objective: we consider the ruined building itself, its age and its history – 'the visible effects of history in terms of decay'. More simply, ruin is part of the general *Weltschmerz, Sehnsucht, malaise*, nostalgia, *Angst*, frustration, sickness, passion of the human soul; it is the eternal symbol. Literature and art have always carried it; it has had, as a fashion, its ups and downs, but the constant mood and appetite is there.

The symptoms do, however, vary at different stages of history and culture; and early in the eighteenth century one charming new symptom emerged. The wind of fashion blew (who can predict when or why it blows?), and it was natural that the active and outdoor British should be blown by it from their contemplation of ruin in pictures and literature and ancient abbeys into their gardens and parks, where they could throw up new ruins of their own. . . . Producing new Tivolis, ruined temples and all, proved an immensely charming occupation for estate-owners, and ruins came into their own as objects in a landscape, picturesque and exciting in themselves and artistic in their relation to the design of the whole.

So began the fashion of building artificial ruins, which raged over Europe through the eighteenth century and well into the nineteenth . . . ruins, classical, Gothic, and even Chinese, sprang up in every fashionable gentleman's grounds, in Great Britain, France, Germany, Austria and the Netherlands . . . garden vistas terminated in ruined objects, classical temples adorned lakes, Baalbek, Palmyra and

Paestum lifted their towers on wooded slopes, Gothic castles, bearing 'the true rust of the Barons' Wars' were commissioned as lodges in parks; cowsheds and dairies, built Roman-ruin-fashion, stood in the cattle yards of *fermes ornées*, landscapes were laid out with ruined temples or abbeys at advantageous points, and ruinated hermitages, complete with hermit, hidden in thickets. It was a delicious game; everyone in the fashionable world played it. . . .

The architects rose to this new opportunity for their skill, and the ruins went up. First the fortified Gothic castles and farms, unruined, like Vanbrugh's fortified buildings at Castle Howard; then Lord Bathurst's Alfred's Hall, a sham ruined castle set in woods in his grounds; there followed sham façades innumerable, rising, blandly and naïvely sly, charmingly and tranquilly hypocritical shells, on what their constructors called eminences. . . . All have the interest of commemorating a period taste, of having once gratified that eternal ruin-appetite which consumes the febrile and fantastic human mind. . . .

The hobby has persisted sporadically into our own day, though our present surfeit of real ruins has now probably halted it. . . . Not that the ruin-craving has past; indeed, its unconscious urge may be working, with inverted zest, to create more of them in all lands. Literature and art are still ruin-grounded; still the bat flits. . . . But it may be hard, in the future, to treat ruins as toys. . . .

New ruins have not yet acquired the weathered patina of age, the true rust of the barons' wars, not yet put on their ivy, nor equipped themselves with the appropriate bestiary of lizards, bats, screech-owls, serpents, speckled toads and little foxes which, as has been so frequently observed by ruin-explorers, hold high revel in the precincts of old ruins (such revelling . . . though noted with pleasure . . . is seldom described in detail; possibly the jackal waltzes with the toad, the lizard with the fox, while the screech-owl supplies the music and they all glory and drink deep among the tumbled capitals). But new ruins are for a time stark and bare, vegetationless and creatureless; blackened and torn, they smell of fire and mortality.

It will not be for long. Very soon trees will be thrusting through the empty window sockets, the rosebay and fennel blossoming within the broken walls, the brambles tangling outside them. Very soon the ruin will be enjungled, engulfed, and the appropriate creatures will revel. Even ruins in city streets will, if they are left alone, come, soon or late, to the same fate. Month by month it grows harder to trace the streets around them; here, we see, is the lane of tangled briars that was a street of warehouses; there, in those jungled caverns stood the large tailor's shop; where those grassy paths cross, a board swings, bearing the name of a tavern. We stumble among stone foundations and fragments of cellar walls, among the ghosts of the exiled merchants and publicans who there carried on their gainful trades. Shells of churches gape emptily; over broken altars the small yellow dandelions make their pattern. All this will presently be; but at first there is only the ruin; a mass of torn, charred prayer books strew the stone floor; the statues, tumbled from their niches, have broken in pieces; rafters and rubble pile knee-deep. But often the ruin has put on, in its catastrophic tipsy chaos, a bizarre new charm. What was last week a drab little house has become a steep flight of stairs winding up in the open between gaily coloured walls, tiled lavatories, interiors bright and intimate like a Dutch picture or a stage set; the stairway climbs up and up, undaunted, to the roofless summit where it meets the sky. The house has put on melodrama; people stop to stare; here is a domestic scene wide open for all to enjoy. Tomorrow or tonight, the gazers feel, their own dwelling may be even as this. Last night the house was scenic; flames leaping to the sky; today it is squalid and *morne*, but out of its dereliction it flaunts the flags of what is left.

The larger ruins are more sad; they have lost more. Nothing can have been more melancholy than the first shattered aspect of the destroyed abbeys before they took on the long patience and endurance of time; they were murdered bodies, their wounds gaped and bled. Their tragedy was like the tragedy of the revolution-destroyed châteaux of France, or the burnt great houses of Ireland, or the cities razed of old by conquerors; the silence brooded heavily round them, as the silence broods over the garden and woods of uprooted Coole. Burnt Hafod crumbled on the mountain like a staunchless grief; Appuldurcombe disintegrated beautifully in all the morbid shades of a fading bruise; Seaton Delaval is sallowed and exquisite in death; Holland House a wrecked Whig dream among gardens. The bombed churches and cathedrals of Europe give us, on the whole, nothing but resentful sadness, like the bombed cities. All the same Monte Cassino put on with wreckage a new dignity, a beauty scarcely in the circumstances bearable; it looked finer than at any time since its last restorations. Caen, Rouen, Coventry, the City churches, the German and Belgian cathedrals, brooded in stark gauntness redeemed only a little by pride; one reflects that with just such pangs of anger and loss people in other centuries looked on those ruins newly made which today have mellowed into ruin *plus beau que la beauté*.

But *Ruinenlust* has come full circle: we have had our fill. Ruin pleasure must be at one remove, softened by art, by Piranesi, Salvator Rosa, Poussin, Claude, Monsù Desiderio, Pannini, Guardi, Robert, James Pryde, John Piper, the ruin-poets, or centuries of time. Ruin must be a fantasy, veiled by the mind's dark imaginings: in the objects that we see before us, we get to agree with St Thomas Aquinas, that *quae enim diminuta sunt, hoc ipso turpia sunt*, and to feel that, in beauty, wholeness is all.

But such wholesome hankerings are, it seems likely, merely a phase of our fearful and fragmented age.

EDITOR'S NOTE

In the selections from Rose Macaulay's text I have preserved the general pattern of her original book, and the titles of the main chapters have been retained, but within this pattern certain rearrangements had to be made. Also in several chapters which relate to many different areas I have made new subsidiary groupings; the titles for them have been chosen from relevant passages in the book itself. The only chapter omitted is that dealing with artificial ruins, 'Art, Fantasy and Affectation'. It was found that a series of photographs of 'Follies' would not combine happily with the remainder of the illustrations, but I have added certain passages from this chapter to Rose Macaulay's concluding 'Note on New Ruins' to form an Epilogue in the present book. Throughout the text I have indicated each point where the sequence of the edited prose diverges from the original by inserting dots.

I have omitted the footnotes which in the original give the sources of many of the quotations, because I assume that readers who intend to pursue these quotations will in any case want to turn to the full edition of the book (it was re-issued by Thames and Hudson in 1966). In the case of a few sites, however, the reader of the present book may wish to know the authorship of descriptions which are quoted without attribution in the text; these are as follows: ruins in the Jebel country on p. 46 (Robin Fedden's *Syria*), Bosra on p. 46 (the *Letters* of Gertrude Bell), the ruined city of Chandravati on p. 80 (James Tod's *Travels in Western India*), Ukheidur on p. 204 (Gertrude Bell's *Amurath to Amurath*).

The original text contains a number of discrepancies of spelling which appear to have resulted from orthographic or typographical confusions; these I have amended, but I have retained unusual spellings where they are recognized alternatives. All dates are given as printed in the original.

My own editorial work is confined to Rose Macaulay's text. The notes on the sites illustrated, and the Index of Plates and Plans, were compiled by members of the publishers' editorial staff, the maps drawn to Roloff Beny's specifications by their art department. The identifications of the photographs are by Mr Beny himself.

C. B. S.

COLOUR PLATES: pp. 9–24

Further details on some of the sites described below will be found in the notes to the black and white plates

9 Columns under water at Hierapolis, Turkey
Marble columns lie scattered in a pool, still fed by the ancient waters, on the flat limestone plateau at Hierapolis. The natural hot springs of the site were used from an early date for religious and medicinal purposes, but the town attained its greatest prosperity in the second and third centuries AD, as is reflected in an inscription of the time: 'Hail golden city Hierapolis; the spot to be preferred before any in wide Asia; revered for the rills of the nymphs; adorned with splendour.'

10 Petra, Jordan. Tomb façade
A towering façade, with attached columns and massive pediment which suggest Hellenistic or Roman influence, is cut in the sandstone rock which encircles Petra. It is one of hundreds of structures, large and small—many of them tombs, some cult monuments perhaps sacred to the god Dushara, and others cave complexes which may have been houses.

11 Babylon, Iraq. View from the desert
Seen from out in the desert, near the waters of the Euphrates, the rebuilt temple of the goddess Nin-mah ('Exalted Lady') rises against the sky. Had Herodotus stood in the same spot when he visited Babylon in the fifth century BC he would have seen also, to the right of the temple, the Gate of Ishtar, the magnificent Palace and Hanging Gardens of Nebuchadnezzar and beyond it the great seven-storey Ziggurat, which was perhaps the Tower of Babel itself, rising 300 feet above street level.

12 Salamis, Cyprus. The Gymnasium
The gymnasium of Salamis (in Cyprus—not to be confused with the island near Athens off which the famous battle was fought), with its colonnades, marble pavements and spacious halls, was so large that when first excavated it was thought to be the *agora* or main public square of the city. The columns seen here are mostly of Byzantine date, though parts of the antique Greek building have been re-used. Every Greek town had its gymnasium (*gymnos* meant 'naked'), which served much the same purpose as the baths of the Romans, though with less emphasis on relaxation and more on exercise.

13 Dawn over the desert city of Palmyra, Syria
The solitary remains of a Graeco-Roman colonnade are silhouetted against the pale sky of a desert dawn at Palmyra. To the English traveller Robert Wood, who visited the site in

1738, the view of such 'Corinthian columns, mixed with so little wall or solid building, afforded a most romantic variety of prospect'.

14 Ninfa, Italy. Green-veiled walls
A broken arch in a buttressed wall, through which a green lane runs; behind, a tumbled dwelling and tall poplars—this is the wild and beautiful domain which is Ninfa today. Since the draining and reclamation of the area over the past century, an enchanting garden has been created around the ruins of the abandoned medieval town by the ducal owners, the Gaetani family.

15 Melrose Abbey, Roxburghshire, Scotland
A mute testament to former glory, rich architectural detail is still visible in this shattered transept from the ruined Cistercian Abbey of Melrose. The present remains of the monastery—long used as a building quarry for its fine red sandstone—chiefly date from its final rebuilding at the turn of the fifteenth century.

16 Copan, Honduras. Stele C
One of the monumental stelae from the Great Court at Copan, stele C, shown in this photograph, is taller than two men. Maudslay found it fallen and overgrown with vegetation. Cleaned and re-erected it revealed an entire human figure on one side and this ruthless bearded face on the other (beards are rare in Mayan art). Below the great face, carved as hanging heads, are death spirits, surrounded by the elaborate symbols of the Mayan hieroglyphic writing. The stele is dated about AD 750.

17 Copan, Honduras. Death's head
The brooding skull, a frequent symbol used in Mayan art, conveys powerfully the terror, suffering and sacrifice which were the basis of their religion. In this photograph it appears as one foot of the stone inner doorway of Temple 22 at Copan.

18 The long-lost city of Machu Picchu, Peru
Spectacularly sited on a mountain ridge whose slopes fall away sharply to the Urubamba gorge 2000 feet below, the fortress-sanctuary of Machu Picchu is seen here with the great peak of Huayna Picchu looming in the background. The nature of the terrain and the need for the Inca refuge to be self-sufficient produced the ingenious system of terracing, which served to retain the moisture and support the soil in which the crops were grown.

19 Haiti. Sans Souci Palace
A palace garden, classical architecture and an ornamental bust suggest the leisured background of eighteenth-century Europe. But this is the West Indian island of Haiti, and its builder was not some nostalgic aristocrat but a negro king, Christophe, the ex-slave who led a revolt against the French in 1806, beat them in battle and established his own independent state. The furniture of his palace was made in Haiti, but most of the marble decoration, pictures and statues he imported from Europe.

20 Banteay Srei, Cambodia. Carved lintel
Still deep in the green jungle, about fourteen miles north-east of fabled Angkor, stands the finest of all the early Khmer temples—the sanctuary of Banteay Srei. Built in the tenth century AD by a Brahmin adviser to the king and dedicated to Siva, its tall stepped shrines and elegant gate-pavilions are covered with a wealth of superb sculptural ornament. On this carved lintel from the top of a portal elephants pour a libation over the goddess Lakshmi, who as the consort of Vishnu is riding on Garuda.

21 Angkor Thom, Cambodia. Finial from a Naga tail
Flanking each of the five approaches to Angkor Thom, monumental sculptures of gods and demons pull on the bodies of two giant Nagas, or serpent deities, whose tails end in finials formed out of smiling faces.

The immense city of Angkor Thom was built around AD 1200 by the last of the great Khmer kings, Jayavarman VII. Much of the complex symbolism of his capital is still imperfectly understood. At one level the scheme of gods, demons and Nagas can be seen as a reworking of the Hindu creation-myth in which the gods and demons used the serpent Sesha to churn the cosmic ocean in their search for the lost elixir of immortality. But for the Khmers the Naga also represented the rainbow—bridge between heaven (here, the sacred city of Angkor Thom) and earth.

22 Medirigiriya, Sri Lanka. The Image-house
Set on their lotus pedestals, Buddha images gaze out serenely from the Image-house at the remote and beautiful monastery of Medirigiriya ('mandala mount') in Sri Lanka. Dated by some scholars to the third century AD, but seemingly a later foundation, Medirigiriya was admired by the historian Raven Hart as the most perfect example of antiquity on the island.

23 Konarak, India. Wheel from the lower platform of the Black Pagoda
Affixed to the base of the Black Pagoda at Konarak, twelve huge wheels of blackened sandstone, each 10 feet in diameter, seem to carry forward the triumphal car of the sun-god, Surya. In front of the car, not visible in the picture, colossal horses are frozen in attitudes of heroic effort as they drag it through the sky.

24 Pagan, Burma. The Shwezigon Pagoda
Three miles north-east of Pagan, overlooking the Irrawaddy River, stands one of the most loved and venerated of all Burmese pagodas whose lavish gilding and exuberant decoration—constantly renewed by the faithful—evoke the dazzling splendour of the former Buddhist capital. According to Burmese chronicles the Shwezigon was built by the unifier of the Pagan empire, King Anawrata: modern research dates the Pagoda slightly later to c. AD 1086 and ascribes its foundation to one of Anawrata's sons, King Kyanzittha, who appears to have built it as a monument to the reformed (Theravada) church in Burma. With its distinctive bell-shaped *stupa* rising 220 feet above ground level, its four smaller surrounding spires and its great sub-base adorned with terracotta bas-reliefs of the Buddha's previous lives the Shwezigon provided a pattern for many later pagodas at Pagan.

INDEX TO PLATES AND PLANS